Transforming Suffering
into Wisdom

The Art of Inner Listening

Applying meditation to everyday life

by
George Kinder

Library of Congress Control Number: 2010916611
ISBN 978-0-9791743-3-9
Copyright © 2010 George D. Kinder
Second Edition

Printed in the United States of America

Serenity Point Press
business@serenitypoint.org
www.serenitypoint.org

Acknowledgements:

Cover photography by George D Kinder
www.georgekinderphotography.com

Cover and book design by Nadine Mazzola
www.nmazzola.com

Illustrations by Gert Lok
Kampen, The Netherlands. www.gertlok.nl

Bert van het Ende
www.uitgeverijrozhanitsa.nl

Kathy Lubar, Joan Luzier, Tom Kinder, Hilary Harts, Drexel Ace, Maryellen Grady, Louis Vollebregt and to my many wonderful students over the years

This book is dedicated to

London and Rachel

Contents

Part Two

Daily Habits and Ordinary Events 93

Relationships 117

Oh that I could leap up to the moon

To dance my delight upon the sky

So nimble is this thrill in my brain

Just from being alive

Preface

W hen I first came to the contemplative life, I came with all the passion of youth to find truth in the wild and untamed territories of spiritual revelation. I was thirsty for mystery and wisdom, and mystical states were my fountain.

But as I grew older, I came to inner work no longer particularly interested in losing myself in its undiscovered and profound landscapes—refuges from the world—but rather because I recognized "the world" lies within me, not only joyous and free, but also fallible, broken, temporal, even uncomfortable and ill at ease— not all the time, but often enough to disrupt my days—this in spite of all the revelations of a mystical life.

And so I became interested in the processes of transformation by which we take the daily broken states of suffering into which we fall, and bring them through their own treacherous landscapes to freedom and a perspective that allows us to alter, not merely the unfortunate circumstance in which we find ourselves, but the very processes by which we arrived there—altering forever how our mind creates suffering and how our actions echo.

For me, this is the process of freedom. The process itself is freedom.

What Is the End of Suffering

For the longest time I wondered, what is the end of suffering? What is its purpose and what is it that arises after it's all over? So often in our lives, we are humbled by it, broken down, even crumpled before it. What if, I wondered, this humbled-down quality, far from being detrimental, was one of the keys to the end of suffering? Isn't humility itself, after all, the cornerstone of wisdom? My mind was filled with questions. What if, in the midst of suffering, we could find a way to enter into suffering's wisdom? How would that look as a practice? What would we do?

The Aspiration to Practice

For years I felt inspired to pursue the end of suffering. Each day I prepared myself as if I were a vessel crafted of four qualities: *dedication, focus, agility and balance*. I would start with an image of the most profound inner practice, however challenging it might be in my life at the time. I would imagine that I was so *dedicated* to knowing who I was, to understanding the world in which I lived and to transforming suffering into wisdom, that I approached every moment of every day as if it was the moment that would bring me to freedom. I would aspire to a *focus* so strong that I might never waver from the object of my inner gaze. And I would strive to be so *agile* that however my mind wandered, I would be fresh and alert to each sensation, each feeling, as if each moment was my child just being born, a song I was just creating. I would imagine a *balance* of attention so developed that whatever change occurred in a moment, I could calibrate just the right degree of effort or ease necessary to meet it—with the delicacy of a hand reaching out to pick up a baby bird.

These four qualities I returned to again and again as I sought to transform my own moments of suffering into wisdom: *dedication, focus, agility* and *balance*. I have certainly seldom done so with such perfection, but nearly always I have approached this work with such aspiration. It is, after all, to me a crucial task, to take the most earthy, unfortunate and uncomfortable raw materials of my own life and

attempt to make of each of them a genuine gem of wisdom, so that I might experience, in moments, again and again throughout my days the transformation of darkness into light. For me the task is crucial because it is what makes all of my life, every moment, worth living.

The exercises you will encounter as you read this book are designed to lead you toward these transformations. They are simple to do, although they take practice. Most of them lead up to, or derive from a concept I call The Structure of Suffering, a notion that each time we are unhappy or we suffer or our world feels out of joint, exactly the same process and structure of thoughts and feelings is occurring inside us. And there is a simple process to unlock that structure of suffering that brings us to freedom. At least it is simple to describe. It takes practice to do well. Altogether I think of the practices of this book as constituting 'the art of inner listening'. It is my hope that as you take on this art, you also will learn how to transform your suffering, whether it feels very small or very large, into wisdom.

Part One

The Three Intentions and Two Pathways to End Suffering

From venturing into my own suffering, I found that three ways in particular stand out as gates of transformation. Each works powerfully on its own. Put them all together, and nothing can stand in their way. They are the three conditions for ending suffering. I call them

The Three Intentions

1. Live in the present moment
2. Pull the plug on the self
3. Be fearless & forgiving in the midst of suffering

Each intention overlaps with the others. You can't really live in the present moment without an absence of self, for instance. And the third intention requires you to both be in the present moment and pull the plug on the self. But each way or intention involves its own unique, genuine and consistent set of practices. Live with these practices and your anxiety will diminish naturally, along with your

despair and your discontent. A sense of inner growth will become palpable each day.

Part One of Transforming Suffering into Wisdom will focus on these three intentions largely as an inner pathway of contemplation and meditation. Part Two will explore an outer pathway of relationship and daily living on which these three means of ending suffering can be practiced. Both pathways provide specific, in depth practices to realize the three intentions.

Intention #1

Live in the Present Moment

I am in a retreat setting. I have taken this week to practice the three intentions, primarily the intention of being present in each moment. It has been hard work, impossible at first, but now I am getting some results, and I am excited and beginning to feel released. Each of my senses has come alive. They are vibrant and sparkle with life. I hardly know how to describe them. Colors are richer, each shift in movement or light carries me into a new world of experience. Sounds are crisper, clearer and more expressive.

There is a bowl of oatmeal with fruit and maple syrup that I pause with for nearly an hour, so tasty and unusual are the sensations of each bite, each movement of the tongue. In an hour, or even in a minute, there are so many more experiences than I've ever had before; none of them is covered over or abstracted by thought. But although each moment feels filled with the richness of life, at the same time there is great quiet and peace pervading my world, as if by watching each moment I am also experiencing a space or spaciousness that exists between moments, or within them.

How I Lost the Present Moment

As I look back now on my life, it strikes me how lucky I was to learn this first intention of presence and delight, or to relearn it.

I'd had many rich moments and much delight as a child. In fact, I recall feeling mostly as if I lived in paradise. But as I grew (or perhaps shrunk) into adulthood, and felt the loss of my childhood paradise, I found myself going more and more into self-absorbed dramas, dreams and fantasies of escape, even resentments and blames that I projected onto the world around me. I felt enslaved by economic circumstances, abandoned by whoever had protected the magic of my childhood and lost and uncertain in my relationships with others. I blamed my family, government and corporations, anything that smacked of adulthood, and all organized communities of action and thought.

It does not matter whether I now disagree or agree with the opinions I then held. What matters is that in attaching to my *thoughts* of how I thought things were, or how I wanted them to be, I was losing what really mattered, the experience of life itself, of how things actually are, which can only be experienced right now, here in this moment.

During this restless period I spent many evenings dabbling in drugs or watching TV. I think now that part of the problem lay in my education. Don't get me wrong. I owe an enormous debt both to my teachers and to the institutions which housed them. I learned many extraordinary things, but, among them, nothing systematic about how to approach the part of my life that was lost. Rather I had learned to be attached to my thoughts and out of touch with my body, with my original nature and with nature itself, and the mystery of its sensations.

> I had been taught that the thoughts and sayings of others were wise, but never instructed how a systematic wisdom could be developed and harvested like grain for rough winters within my own body.

Adding to my challenge, I was raised in a family of lawyers, where I learned to be attached to opinions and to judge every circumstance of life for its right and its wrong.

As a consequence I felt lost to myself, unhappy, judgmental and vulnerable to the world. Yet through all this I kept in my mind a primary image, stronger than all the others. It was of the 'paradise' of my childhood, and of the wisdom of the many teachers who came before us. I was determined to find my way back there, and I dedicated a portion of each day to inner practice and to cultivating awareness of the present moment. How fortunate I now feel that this seed of practice rose above the weeds of my discontent and flourished for me into a way of life.

The Meditation Object

The present moment is an incredible object for the art of inner listening because it is always with us. It's always right here. You never have to go rummaging around looking for it. It's also challenging, exciting and invigorating because it never stays still. It's never the same. Learning to be with it thus adds vitality to our lives. It aids us in our work to transform suffering into wisdom because if we can stay with the present moment, that means we can experience our suffering directly (as much as our excitement or our joy), and thus are in a better position to work with it.

> Trying to resolve our suffering without being with it moment by moment is like trying to do surgery without the patient in the room.

It is possible, and enriching, to seek to stay present with every experience in our lives: with sports, eating, reading, walking, partying, working, loving, even sleeping. But if we want to get better and better at being present, it is useful to have a repetitive practice, within a narrow range, to keep returning to again and again. This practice will give us greater skill to meet any moment in our lives.

You can practice being present with any sense base; with taste, smell, sight or hearing. But for inner listening, the best is the experience of touch, inside your self. It is just simply closer to a full-bodied sense of who we are: troubled or dear, vulnerable or excited, hungry, loving or exhausted. Simply put, while often neutral in feeling, the sense of touch is closer to our joy and closer to our suffering than any other sense base.

So, it will be useful if our meditation object is found in the sense-base of touch, narrowly confined and clear to sense. If it is so, we will know directly when we are meeting or not meeting our meditation object with our awareness. Our focus can be both contained and concentrated.

Given these criteria, the breath as experienced in the belly or possibly the nostrils, is an excellent choice.

Inner Listening Instructions

Whether you sit on a cushion, a bench, or a straight-back chair, find a posture where your back is erect, your body relaxed, and you feel confident you can sit still without moving for the length of the meditation.

Try not to move even for an itch, or a pain in the back. Unless you feel that you are actually harming the body, keep still. You will find that a still posture will sharpen your concentration and produce deeper meditations. Every time you adjust the posture, whether from anxiety, discomfort or to scratch, you break your concentration. Often it will feel as if you have to start the meditation all over again.

Bring your attention to the physical sensations of breathing, either at your nostrils or at your belly. Relax into the rhythm of the breath, experiencing the sensations of the belly expanding and contracting, or of the air rushing into the nostrils and then easing out. As you relax, see if you can sharpen your attention to the beginnings and endings of sensations as you follow the breath from the beginning of the in-breath to the ending of the out-breath. Don't try to control the breath.

> It doesn't matter what the breath does. We are training the mind, not the breath, to be nimble, fresh, clear and at ease.

Notice the qualities of sensations. You might take a minute, for instance, and just notice the shape of your sensations, as you breathe in, as you breathe out. Not how you imagine or see a shape, but what shape the breath actually feels like as it enters and exits the nostrils or the belly. It might not feel like what you think of as a shape. It might feel like an irregular line coursing through the body, changing shapes as it goes. Or it might feel like tiny points of sensation in space, evaporating as they arise. Or it might be a two- or three-dimensional object, full-bodied with breath. Whatever shape the breath feels like, follow it for a while, alert to its changes.

Then take a minute and notice how the breath moves, moment by moment. Does the breath twirl through the nostrils or belly, or is the movement slow but inexorable? Does the breath leap from sensation to sensation, or is it stationary? For another minute, see if you can identify temperature differences between the in-breath and the out-breath. Then, just notice the feeling-quality itself: the quality of hardness (harshness) or softness, pressure, tension or ease, the sense of contact as the breath makes its rounds in the nostrils or the belly.

And finally, staying as nimble and as fresh as you can, simply notice, with ease, whatever sensations are arising.

Whenever a thought arises, let it go and return to the breath. No matter how alluring or annoying the thought might be, as soon as you notice you are thinking, return to the breath, gently, and without judgment. Continue to return directly to your breath

throughout your meditation, whenever you find your awareness has wandered from it.

You will have "good" meditations where you will feel very peaceful, or where you will experience states of bliss, or where you will follow every nuance of breath with a clarity and alertness that seems uncanny. And you will have "bad" meditations where restless with thought or overwhelmed with lethargy you are only able to return to the breath twice in an entire meditation.

In reality, a bad meditation is a "good" meditation; it's where we do the work.

What we are doing in meditation is retraining the mind to no longer follow the deep habits of stress, suffering or neurosis that we normally follow. When we are filled with turmoil, and we manage even twice to return to the breath, we send a message to our unconscious that it is no longer in charge, that we will choose to be present, alert and at ease, rather than follow our unconscious habits into fantasy or into suffering, that the days of these unconscious patterns are numbered.

A "good" meditation is useful, too. It may inspire us to continue to meditate when times get tough. A good meditation is often the fruition of the efforts we've made in meditation to be present.

Fine Tuning Intention

It can be helpful to work with intention as we begin our approach to inner listening. A clear or inspired intention can make the difference between a murky meditation and one that is nimble and alert. You could choose any of the Three Intentions as you begin your meditation. But it will be particularly useful to fine tune the First Intention *to live in the present moment*.

At the beginning of your meditation, form the intention of bringing your awareness as close to the physical sensations of breathing as possible in every moment. If you have had successful meditations in the past, remember how it felt as your awareness nuzzled up to your breath. Remember also you are working with intention, not will power. The most effective intention often carries the lightest touch. If you lose track of the breath in your meditation, be gentle with yourself as you come back first to your intention and then to the breath.

Another way to use intention is to review the kinds of things that happen when you miss the breath in a meditation. For instance, do you space out or find yourself in a trance? Do you run a side commentary on your performance as a meditator while you are meditating? Or do you get lost in stories of escape or of the day to come? Remind yourself of these patterns, as you prepare to meditate, and form the intention of bringing your awareness back from these diversions, not to get lost in them, back to the breath with all its changes and sensations.

Another way to use intention is to remind yourself as you begin your practice, that meeting each and every moment as it arises and passes away is the path to freedom.

Inner Listening:
Times and Fruits

Meditate a minimum of 20 minutes a day and you will have
established a firm foundation in the ways that end suffering. Do it
an hour a day and you will begin to learn as much about yourself
and the way things are as you would from any study of philosophy
or religion. At 2-3 hours a day you will notice palpable changes
in your understanding and depth, your demeanor and actions
on a daily basis. And if you were to practice like a monk in the
mountains, 3-5 hours a day you would begin to live as if your whole
life were filled with blessing and with truth.

There is no need for you to look anywhere outside of your own
experience in this moment to find the truth.

Notice that when you follow the physical sensations of breathing, at
least two of the three ways to end suffering, 'the Three Intentions'
are automatically happening. First, you are living in the present
moment. Second, you have pulled the plug on the self. As you
strengthen your practice, you will find the third way, the way of being
fearless and forgiving in the midst of suffering, arising naturally in
your meditations as well.

Moments Arise,
Moments Pass Away

As your practice gets strong, you will actually experience individual moments of sensation arising and passing away.

If you primarily watch moments arising, life is exciting, dramatic, electric, vital, mysterious, ever changing, sparkling with life, vigorous, creative, and most often delightful.

If you primarily watch moments leaving, life is more sorrowful. You experience everything passing away.

If you manage to catch the middle of moments as they pass through your awareness, you see everything, and it is complete and whole, empty of self but all encompassing. It is as if you are the complete human being, the universal being, and all is as it is meant to be in the world.

Moving On

As we become stronger at the First Intention of *Living in the Present Moment*, we awaken to and live in all our senses, even more than in our thoughts. We experience the texture and fragrance of life – rich, emotive, whole, complete – sparkling, crackling with energy and vitality--how things are, how they actually are without the intermediation of thought or of self. To experience this is part of the process of transforming suffering into wisdom. How else, but by learning to be present, can we see suffering for what it is?

Tasting, touching, smelling, hearing, seeing and all that come with them. To me there is nothing richer and more pulsing, energizing and alive than the experience of this intention. The other two intentions don't always present themselves. *Pull the plug on the Self?* Well, the 'I-thoughts' that construct the self are not always there, not in every moment. And suffering (*to be fearless and forgiving in the midst of suffering*) is likewise not always there.

Of the three intentions, *"to live in the present moment"* is the simplest to understand and the most universal (the present moment is always here). It is the foundation on which all the rest of our work will be based.

Transforming Suffering into Wisdom

Intention #2
Pull the Plug on the Self:
Wood Valley

I am walking down the mountain road at Wood Valley on the Big Island of Hawaii in the spring time. The sun is bright, each shadow dark and the fragrance of wild ginger floats in the breeze. The wild, melodic cries of Hawaiian cardinals follow me as each foot falls like a sack of rocks to the earth, grounded in the earth, till the next foot lifts like rapid water racing over rocks to fall to the earth once again. My breath is measured by the rhythm of the feet. My gaze is on the changing contours of the ground.

My inward gaze is fresh to each changing moment, moment after moment all along the mountain road, when suddenly I realize I am experiencing something deep within, something that knows how to be complete in each moment and alive, something that feels like integrity, not as that brittle place inside us known as "taking a stand," clinging to an opinion, a place already broken because wounded and defended, but rather an uprushing of energy from each footfall, up the legs and the spine and flourishing out the top of the head like swaying branches with the strength of a stallion uprearing in arousal.

And I'm walking down the road astonished at this newfound energy, this uncluttered and unobstructed self-knowing, when I suddenly notice I have *intermittent thoughts with this experience, thoughts of my childhood, thoughts of my business, thoughts of my home. And every time one of these thoughts comes by, not only does an opaque curtain fall between me and the whole scene I am in, but I lose these waters of integrity rushing through my limbs as well. Stay in the present moment, free of thoughts of the self, and integrity flourishes through my body, a wild wind bringing all the creatures and plants of the rainforest to life. Thoughts of self arise, and my being is broken. It's like a desert storm parched of life.*

Self and Freedom from Self

The Self seems all pervasive. We carry on a constant conversation with ourselves, and from ourselves to the world. Yet how beautiful it can be, we have already seen, to be free of its endless repetitions, how much more present we can be and in the moment.

So many things are impossible, or very difficult without a freedom from self. For instance, how can you experience a fullness of heart without emptying yourself? How can you play beautiful music, or even play genuinely with another? Sure, I know, some of you are thinking, "What about those rock stars? Don't they have a lot of ego?" Perhaps, but keep in mind, we are talking about the "Self" as the "I-thoughts" that arise to cloud our experience.

> The rock star could invite a swarm of I-thoughts after her performance, but during the performance she'd better lose her "self" in the music, or she'll lose the melody or the beat or the connection of her heart to her sound.

As soon as our stories of ourselves intervene, trouble comes calling. We blank out to the richness of experience in order to follow, rehearse or attach to story lines in a plot.

We have seen in our discussion of the First Intention, how free we become of the self when we are present with each moment. To see completely clearly in every situation, with none of our self-preoccupations intruding, how freeing! How masterful!

Freedom from self and all our stories of our selves brings a great relief, a deep quiet, a stillness, a profound sense of peace.

Creating the Self as Something to Hold Onto

There are many ways we create the self, calling it, with our "I-thoughts" our "my-thoughts", our "me-thoughts" into being. One of the times we bring the self into being is when we want to avoid feeling anxious.

Perhaps we just developed a crush on our boss, or suspect our landlord wants us out. Rather than learn the third intention of being fearless and forgiving in the midst of our anxiety, we plunge into stories of our selves filled with images of love or loss, of power or defeat instead.

> The self becomes a way to escape, to protect us from our uncomfortable feelings, but the cost is immense. In the tedium of our stories, we lose all of our freshness, our vitality, even our life.

We also create a self as a way to seek consolation, or safety in something permanent. Perhaps we just had a wonderful evening that we want to hold onto, or we recall again and again some accomplishment we had during the week at work. But even here, by clinging to this self we lose the present moment and the nature of how things are, how each moment changes. We cling to an illusion, to what is past, what is abstract and no longer true – or alive.

Another way the self can rob us of the present moment is when we find ourselves protecting our image rather than living authentically. Whether it's a job interview or someone just coming into our space, we cling to who we think we ought to be in relation to them, and become disappointed or angry that we can't live up to our image or that we can't be ourselves. We can plague ourselves with endless self-judgments.

Soon enough if we study the self we discover that selfing is tedious, while the present moment is tasty. Even anxiety can become tasty practicing the second intention. So, how can we *pull the plug on our self* without getting lost or alienated? How do we actually do the practice?

How We Pull the Plug On the Self

We pull the plug on ourselves all the time. How does it happen? Coming home from work is a good example. Unwinding from all the pressures of the day might just as easily be called "unselfing".

We do it by reading the newspaper, cooking a meal, turning on the TV, taking a walk, or talking about things with our friends, until our wound-up urge to identify with everything that went right or wrong during the day has been unwound.

There is a more direct way. Although difficult at first, with practice it becomes second nature. It is very simple. As soon as you notice a thought of I, me or mine, let go of that thought and return to the present moment. Return to your senses. Come back to the experience of who you are in the moment, rather than the concept or story of who you are. Trust the process; it will keep taking you exactly where you need to go, revealing as you go, more and more subtle layers and levels of yourself.

But What Happens to Me?

You might wonder, "What happens to me if I pull the plug on the
self, will my life dry up, will I feel lonely or alienated, what happens
to my self, my dreams, my relationships, my place in the world?"
Perhaps the surprising thing is that nothing but good happens from
pulling the plug on the self. Nothing but deepening, strength and a
new-found clarity. It's not always easy. Giving up a habit is never
easy. And new darknesses will emerge within the clarity, darknesses
that will have their own "I-thoughts" to let go of. What diminishes
will be your clinging as all the places you cling to are released from
your anxious grip.

> Instead of limiting your self-experience to narrow, grasping,
> repetitive reminders of who you are, you experience life
> itself rushing through your veins.

All those things about you that are familiar or that you love remain:
your talents, your interests, your accomplishments, your history and
memories, your passions, your connections, your inclinations and
your dreams as well as the richness of your senses. What you have
shifted is an ego structure that is grasping and clinging to one that
is at ease and sees things clearly, from a being that often contracts in
suffering to one that feels more connected with the world around it.

Flush with life itself, when you see suffering around you, you know how to relieve it.

Pull the plug on the self and you will see. You are life itself, and not a diminished thing.

Selfless Action

Action and inaction: In both be selfless.

As we learn to pull the plug on the self, we reap an intrinsic gift. In freeing ourselves of our greatest burden, we naturally become more generous in our actions and find ourselves modeling "non-grasping" behavior, something sorely wanting in our world.

It is not that we don't act with directness, power or conviction. Quite to the contrary. For instance, our ability to set boundaries or limits is far more effective, unburdened of the taint of selfing.

> Rather we find our actions
> more accomplished because more flexible
> more energized because less brittle
> more clear because less attached.

The Misery of the World

When we pull the plug on the self, we come mysteriously in touch with the universality of suffering—how our own misery is no different from the misery of the world, nor from the misery of any other creature in it. Our compassion grows. At the same time, no longer preoccupied with the weary grandiosity of ourselves, we see how our suffering is no different from individual sensations of discomfort arising and passing away within us. And as we watch free of the preoccupations of self, but present to every moment, we find that these sensations form a tapestry or quilt that comforts us sensation by sensation in our dismay. Each time we pull the plug on our self and return to these sensations, we are practicing with the second and first intentions and we've begun our practice with the third intention, as well.

As we mature in the practice, we realize how often we can let the "self" go in our daily lives, how often in fact it is the stories with "I" in them that make us anxious and neurotic, and how simple it becomes just to let them go. They're not what matters. Being present is what matters, and being fearless and forgiving in the midst of suffering is what matters, and being free of self.

Meditation on Pain

Before we move on to the third intention of being fearless and forgiving in the midst of suffering, it will be useful to consider how to do an inner listening practice in the midst of Pain, and to consider how the self gets in the way of our freedom when Pain is around. Often we confuse pain with suffering. So in your next meditation, notice what happens when Pain arises.

At first, when you meet each breath, sensation by sensation, you sail along free of the self that leads to suffering, fresh to every moment.

A Pain or an itch arises and: "This is uncomfortable [to me]," "I don't like this," "What can I do to change this?" "I'll just scratch or move". The "I" arises with the pain, the present moment is entirely lost in self-centered stories, and there you are anxious and annoyed by suffering. The three ways to end suffering are suddenly all absent from your life.

Try this instead.

> Remember, freedom from suffering is not a zone we achieve or live in, but rather is a process that is alive, alert, fresh and nimble in each moment.

When pain arises, notice it the way you notice the breath, sensation by sensation. Let your "I" thoughts go. If the pain or itch does not indicate real harm to the body, then either let the pain go and return to the breath or let the breath go, making the pain or itch your meditation object until it no longer distresses you. It takes a true fearlessness to keep letting go of a plague of I-thoughts, while returning to the painful sensations as your object of meditation. When you pay attention to these sensations, you realize they are constantly changing and what started as painful may become merely interesting (what does throbbing really feel like) or even, strangely enough, pleasurable and eventually may disappear all together.

Of course if the pain does indicate real harm to the body it may make sense to shift your posture or to see a doctor. The three intentions are helpful in bringing an end to suffering. They have a more limited capacity to reduce pain and its underlying conditions.

Transforming Suffering into Wisdom

Intention #3

Be Fearless and Forgiving In the
Midst of Suffering

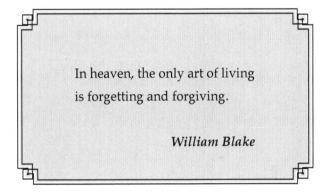

In heaven, the only art of living
is forgetting and forgiving.

William Blake

Searching the Sea for Moments of Time

I catch so many moments
of guilt, of fear, of shame
as I walk across the sand

Like a warrior
catching arrows of delight
I place them in my quiver
And search out across the waters
roiling at my ankles
for my prey

A Song for Hana
George Kinder

Now that we have studied them all
[the passions] we see that we have
much less reason to fear them than
before. For we see that they are all
good by nature and all we need do is
avoid their excess or bad uses.

And these can be cured by separating
in oneself the motions of the blood and
spirits from the ideas they are usually
linked with.

Descartes, Treatise on the Passions
Translator Barzun

Betrayal

*I am at work. It is the middle of the day, and I discover, in an inadvertent
phone call, that I have been betrayed by a close friend. This is a friendship
I have been pleased to have, and that has been growing closer over the past
few months. As soon as I can get out of the office I leave and drive home.
My mind is overwhelmed with confusion, a jumble of stories, questions and
feelings. In shock, I can't focus, but I am eager to get home, where I know I
will immediately do the practice of the third intention.*

*I pull into the driveway, drop all the contents of my work in the kitchen, and
rush out to my back porch. There I begin to pace. I have too much energy in
my body to tolerate sitting, but, regardless, I know that in every moment I
must let my thoughts go, and focus precisely, exclusively and fearlessly on
the feelings in my body.*

*For an hour I pace back and forth, rapidly and without rest. Each time
a thought arises, I let it go, but my mind is a swarm of thoughts, each of
them glued it seems to a gut wrenching feeling. Sorrow at the loss of my
friendship, anger at the betrayal, indignation at the details of the situation,
despair and anxiety as I consider what I might do next. And each time one
of these thoughts arises, I let it go, separating it from the feelings, and bring
my fierce focus back to how the feelings feel in my body, to the sorrow in the
lump in my throat, to the despair which feels like nausea in my belly, to the
rage that seems to impetuously and rapidly move my limbs through the cool
air across the porch, to a scream ready to be launched between my jaw and*

my ears. At one point, I am so lost in rage, I have the image of Macbeth and murder in my mind. And that too, I let go to feel the underlying feelings, and how the feelings shift in my body, accumulating space, roiling, changing location, and then finally coming down to a fire of rage in my belly, much of my energy spent. I sit down, half relieved, but no less focused and intent on meeting each moment of rage. I know I'm not finished. I have been fearless with my attention, but as I sit, I feel forgiveness inside me, toward myself as much as my friend. And as I feel the burning sense of fire still fierce in my stomach, I can see its flame rising into my chest, filling my torso. As the flames grow more precise in my feeling observation, something strange happens. An aroma of roses begins to surround me. The fire begins to smolder, and the smoldering red ashes assume the shape of red roses, rising up out of my belly and into my chest. The fire of rage becomes completely subsumed by the bouquet of roses and its aroma, and disappears into it. I am done, spent, and free.

There is no more anger in me, no more thoughts or stories to rehearse. I am weary, if at peace. I realize that it is all about the other person, now, not me. There is nothing that I need to do, other than possibly set a limit or a boundary in my relationship next time we meet. But the real realization is of the power of the Third Intention, to be fearless and forgiving in the midst of suffering. Something that might have taken me weeks to get through, was over in an hour.

Swamp of Mud
Seed of Wisdom

> The most extraordinary thing about suffering is that it has a structure and the structure of suffering is the key to its unraveling and to its wisdom.

When we hear the word, suffering, we can imagine something intractable, a swamp of mud that extends for a thousand miles in all directions, something that has caught everyone in its morass.

But suffering is much simpler than this. It can be distinguished from pain. It can be isolated in a moment. It can be cut into its facets like a diamond and opened like a seed of wisdom.

The Structure of Suffering

The structure of suffering is quite simple. And each time we suffer it's exactly the same. When you realize this you wonder, why do we keep doing it? Think about the very last time you were really upset about something, and see if this isn't true.

There are **three** elements to a structure of suffering.

1. First of all, there is a jumble of uncomfortable feelings. Sometimes it's just one feeling, like anger. At other times it's a mix of feelings all roiled together that might include sadness, fear, humiliation, despair, anxiety and frustration among others.

2. On top of our feelings, there is a series of thoughts, judgments, opinions or stories about our suffering, about ourselves or others, that get hooked to our uncomfortable feelings. (Some say they cause our feelings.)

3. Finally, the lynch-pin that hooks our thoughts to our feelings is me, I and mine. The stories, consciously or unconsciously, are inevitably about me, or offend me and mine. There is a sense that these thoughts and feelings are an intimate, if troubled, part of our identity in each moment of suffering.

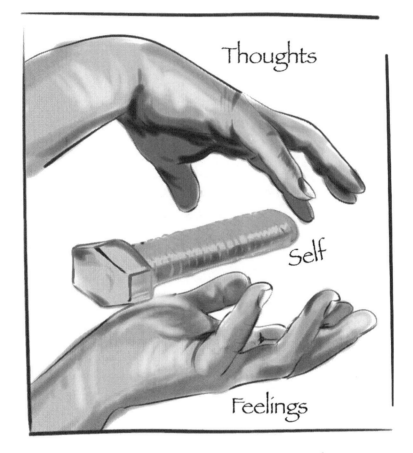

There is a simple practice to end suffering, simple to describe at least, although much more difficult to do. I call it:

Letting Thoughts Go,

Letting Feelings Be

We will explore the structure of suffering and its release in some depth throughout this section of the book.

Suffering's Depravity and Nobility

There is a quality of depravity or of pathos to suffering needlessly, to wasting our life in suffering.

But to face the suffering we encounter, unflinching, to unravel its strands, and while letting its stories go, to be present with its physical sensations and feelings, this is a Noble life, courageous and compassionate.

> What could be more courageous than to face directly the darkest moments of suffering? What could be more noble than to transform suffering into wisdom?

It is a mission that is accomplished by practicing the three intentions of *living in the present moment, pulling the plug on the self, and being fearless and forgiving in suffering's midst.*

Suffering Is Unbearable

A moment of suffering itself is unbearable.

That is to say, we leap to something else when we suffer (T.V., refrigerator, telephone, email, alcohol, lovers, the mall, complaints, resentments and blames, projections and introjections) rather than experience in a clear way what suffering actually is, what it feels like, and how it's constructed. Rather than experience it, we get lost in it.

Suffering is unbearable regardless of its intensity. Once we have succumbed to its cloying structure of feelings, thoughts and self, we blank out, we don't see things clearly and we seek to escape. Granted, some suffering is more physically painful than others, some suffering is more intense. But whether we suffer from high fever, starvation, torture or the threat of death, or from someone spiking our tires, spilling a plate of food on our laps, or selling us a lemon instead of an orange, the structure of suffering is the same and the path to its release inside ourselves is the same.

The Practice

We learn about suffering, including the greatest of sufferings, just by observing our own small measures of suffering each time they arise.

How do we use a practice of observation to come to suffering's wisdom? There are three steps:

- First, recognize when you're suffering. See it as a bell of awakening.
- Second, identify the structure of suffering. Learn to distinguish clearly between its three elements of feelings, thoughts and self.
- Third, practice letting thoughts go, letting feelings be.

Take these three steps and you will learn how both pain and feelings are different from suffering. How staying present with your emotions while letting your thoughts and stories go, you no longer feel "stuck" in suffering. Watch how the "sticky" glue of the ego is pulled out and dissolves when we learn to rest in the feelings themselves, being present in every moment.

The Bell of Awakening

For centuries philosophers have asked: If there is a god, how can there be so much suffering?

It seems an inevitable part of the biological world we live in that there is birth and death. And where there is death, infirmity, disease and old age (not to mention adolescence) we expect there to be suffering.

But whereas death is a fact of life, suffering is not. Suffering involves how we experience and take personally the fallibility of the world we live in and the bodies we occupy, the disappointments and the pains. Without the self hooking our uncomfortable feelings to our relentless thinking, there is no personal suffering, there are only feelings and what we experience as pain becomes mere sensations.

Suffering is here for a purpose.
It is calling out to us
we have fallen from our path,
lost our center.

SUFFERING IS THE BELL OF AWAKENING

calling us back to the three ways that end suffering: to living in the present moment, to pulling the plug on the self, and to being fearless and forgiving in the midst of suffering.

Whenever you find yourself suffering, don't race to the refrigerator, the web, the telephone or the mall. Take stock of yourself. Ask yourself: am I practicing the three intentions or am I lost in confusion and struggle? Return to your practice. Bring a genuine end to suffering.

Letting Thoughts Go, Letting Feelings Be

Letting thoughts go, letting feelings be unravels the knot of suffering. If we are truly effective in this practice, or if it becomes second nature to us, we can break the pattern of suffering forever. A pattern that we keep returning to, a repetitive dream that has become a nightmare.

Did you ever wonder why you keep returning to the well of suffering? A mere child only has to touch a hot stove once to know never to touch it again. Yet how many times have we had to touch the searing qualities of anger, fear, humiliation or despair? Will we never learn?

What we didn't know as children when we were sent to our rooms and rehearsed messages ("I'll show you" or "I hate you" or "How could I be such an idiot?" and many others) was that these burning qualities of anger, fear, humiliation and despair harmed us only if we clung to our stories and to the ego that attached to them. Otherwise, these feelings burned like wisdom through our souls. God doesn't speak English. Divinity reveals itself in how the wild and untamed inside us comes to peace, how the unruly motions of the heart or the chaos of nature finds meaning as it breaks into human song. We can't hear this without paying attention. *Letting thoughts go, letting feelings be* is a way of becoming aware of exactly how this transformation takes place, and thus becoming masters of it. Accomplished musicians of the spirit. The tragedy of our childhood lies in what we didn't know. What we were rehearsing up in our rooms was the structure of suffering, not how to free ourselves from it, so that it became a habit so deeply engrained that even now, years into adulthood, we are just beginning to learn how to end it.

Recall the structure of suffering: a jumble of uncomfortable feelings hooked to our thoughts and stories by the lynch-pin of I, me and mine. When we let thoughts go and let our feelings be, we make our feelings into an object of contemplation, returning to them moment by moment, with care and fortitude (fearless and forgiving) regardless of the messages, thoughts or stories that get in our way. We simply let these thoughts go and when we let our thoughts go, it seems, as if by magic, our I, me and mine diminishes as well. Then return to the pure feelings underlying them, until something we might call Understanding arises and we feel at ease, no longer troubled by our suffering.

You can see how the three intentions are all working together here. We are *living in the present moment*, sensation by sensation in our feelings. We are *pulling the plug on our self* as we let our thoughts go. And we are *being fearless and forgiving in the midst of suffering* in our direct approach to the troublesome feelings.

Meditation on Suffering

When we find ourselves suffering in a meditation, our first practice
is to simply return to the breath. If you are capable of remaining
with the breath for even half of its duration, this is generally the best
practice. Notice that your mind has wandered and return to
the breath.

If, on the other hand, you find that after numerous attempts when
you return to the breath it is only for a split second and then you are
lost again in your suffering, it is time to work with the third intention
to be fearless and forgiving in the midst of suffering, to let thoughts
go and let feelings be. See if you can shift your awareness from the
breath to the emotion that is embedded in the structure of suffering
you are experiencing. See if you can find the emotion in the body
and bring all of your attention to its qualities and its changing
sensations. Continue to let your thoughts go while you bring your
full meditative awareness to the feelings. Stay with the feelings until
the suffering itself no longer plagues you. At that point, return to
the breath.

Attempting for too long to stay with the breath when a structure of
suffering won't let you ends up repressing a feeling that will only
come back more fiercely to haunt you later on. By shifting your
focus to the feeling itself, free from thoughts, you will disarm the
structure of suffering and decondition future structures. What's

more, what your suffering is saying to you is that the only way to live in the present moment is to be with your feelings until they are no longer interested in clinging to your thoughts.

There are three guises I use to do this practice. I call them The Scientist, The Compassionate Mother and The Warrior Scout.

The Scientist

The scientist is interested in the facts, and in understanding how things are constructed, how they work.

So, in relation to suffering, having let the thoughts go and observed the "I" diminish, what remains?

> What are the feelings that remain?
> Can I name them as single-word emotions?
> Where are they in the body?
> What do they actually feel like?

Feelings

Most feelings that remain after letting our thoughts go are variations on our three primary aversive emotions: anger, sadness and fear. These feelings include: anxiety, frustration, depression, despair, shame, guilt, rage and humiliation. There are also feelings that remain from our desirous emotions, among them yearning, envy, jealousy, greed, hunger, lust. Or we may feel bored, dull, sleepy, lethargic. Occasionally even our positive feelings of joy, excitement and love can trap us in structures of suffering when we attempt to bind them to ourselves.

Location of Feelings

Generally we find our feelings in sensations of the upper half of our body, from the waist up: in our stomach, chest, neck, shoulders, back, arms, fists, fingers, throat, jaw, mouth, cheeks and eyes.

Occasionally, we find emotion located in the lower half of the body (thus the expression "weak in the knees", for instance): groin, hips, thighs, knees, calves, feet, toes.

Often, particularly if we're new to this practice, we may not be able to locate our feelings in the body at all.

Sensations

If we feel our emotions with the dispassion of a scientist, we will find that they generally have characteristics in the body of shape and dimension, temperature, movement and a feeling quality, and that they are constantly, if subtly, changing.

Shape

Does our emotion feel like a point or points in space, or does it have a single dimension as a line does? If it feels like a line, is it a straight line, curved or irregular in shape? Or is our feeling felt as a flat object, a circle, oval, square, rectangle or an irregular flat shape – a surface? Or is it a three-dimensional object with rounded or sharp edges? Is it irregular in shape?

Dimension

Does our feeling occupy the whole body, or the upper half of the body, or the whole belly? Or does it occupy just a finger's length or a mere point in space?

Temperature

Sometimes our anger feels like a fire in the belly, our fear like a chill running up and down the spine. What qualities or range of temperature do you feel as you observe the physical sensations that manifest when you feel a feeling? Or does the temperature feel neutral, not there?

Movement

Are the sensations moving about, or are they stationary? Do they have a direction, a beginning or an ending? Are they moving rapidly, slowly? Do they disappear and return? Are they throbbing, pulsating, gurgling or vibrating? Do they feel shaky?

Feeling Quality, Texture

Is there a harshness or a softness to the feeling? Does it feel faint or clear, hard, sharp or blunt? Twisting, tight, rough, smooth, loose or at ease? Does it feel nauseous or tense?

Conclusion

The scientist attempts to name, locate and observe whatever feelings arise in the body, staying with the sensations for as long as they are manifesting, or at least as long as they trouble us by hooking themselves onto our stories and our identities.

You will find that there is no need to stay any longer than that, nor to do any other action than simple observation. Just living in the present moment is enough. Of course the scientist is doing two of the other actions that end suffering as well: he's pulling the plug on the self by not giving it energy, not paying attention to it. (He is paying close attention to the feelings, not the self's stories.) And by hanging in there with the difficult feelings, attempting to observe them as mere sensations, he's being fearless in the midst of suffering.

"But I don't..."

"But I don't have feelings. I'm not a feeling kind of person. And I'm not sure I want to feel them if they are there. The only feelings I feel are in my head. If I do feel a feeling, it certainly isn't located in sensations in my body!"

Sometimes it can take as long as a couple of years to even find a feeling in the body. That's okay. We can still pull the plug on the self, live in the present moment and be fearless and forgiving in the midst of suffering, *while we're searching the body for feelings.*

And as for not wanting to feel your feelings, why not? Don't you feel feelings when you listen to music? Of course you do. And most of the time music and feelings feel rich and rewarding. Well, feelings are our music. Why would you not want to know them, intimately and in detail? To know yourself that richly, that deeply?

Aristotle described how theatre works for each of us by giving us the opportunity to experience tragic feelings directly and cathartically,

how we have a transformative experience with the darkest feelings, because in theatre (or movies), the story is not about us. This is also the magic of the three intentions. By pulling the plug on ourselves our feelings become cathartic, and our personal dramas lead to the rich music of freedom, rather than to swamps of suffering.

Here's What I Suggest

Most of us are aware of experiencing three or four feelings on a daily basis, even if we don't find them as sensations in the body. Let's say the feelings you feel most often are anger, frustration, anxiety, guilt and depression.

The next time you feel one of these feelings, pause and look in your body to see if it feels different from the times you feel peaceful, at ease, happy and clear. Often we will feel greater tension in some part of the body, or we'll feel movement or sensations of energy. Just look and see. If you experience nothing, go back to your other practices.

Eventually this practice will open up for you the whole range of feelings that you have. Most likely it will occur in a crisis when your feelings are most powerful. You might wonder again, "Why do I want to feel all those feelings? I just want them to go away." But what we really want to go away is the suffering, and as long as our feelings are hidden from us, we will unconsciously hook them to our thoughts and identify with them, producing suffering endlessly throughout our lives.

At first we may find these feelings quite uncomfortable, but as we practice the three guises of The Scientist, The Mother and The Warrior Scout, we come to a place of peace and forgiveness with the feelings. They become like old shoes; they may not be chic, may smell a bit, but they are both familiar and comfortable. We even find some kindly affection for them.

So if you find yourself in a structure of suffering, and you have let the thoughts go, hang in there with the feelings, let them be. Observe them, live with them separate from your thoughts and stories, just as sensations in the body. You are a scientist exploring the nature of suffering and how to end it. No matter how uncomfortable, watch every moment of sensation, while letting your thoughts and identification go.

If you feel the practice is too cold or antiseptic for you and you're feeling lonely for a kind friend, it is time to practice the second guise, that of the compassionate mother.

The Compassionate Mother or the Practice of Kindness

As we shift in our practice (of the present moment) from the observation of mere sensations to the observation of sensations tinged with emotion, we may be overwhelmed by the unbearability of suffering and find ourselves trapped again and again in its maze of feeling, story, and self. We may find ourselves overwhelmed by loneliness and unable, alone, to let go of our stories, and stay steady in our vigil of feeling our most difficult feelings and the apparent darkness of our souls. We may find ourselves saying horrible things to ourselves, unspeakable judgments that we would never say to our child or to a friend who is in pain. Here we must learn to become our own best friend.

It is in these circumstances that the second guise in the practice of letting feelings be finds its necessary place. This is the guise of the mother with her only child.

If the scientist and the warrior bring fearlessness right to the face of suffering, the compassionate mother bears forgiveness. When her only child comes crying to her, she drops everything to bring a touch of kindness to her troubled daughter or son.

The practice of kindness in the midst of a structure of suffering goes much the same way. We drop entirely our thoughts and stories and all our preoccupations to bring a touch of kindness to our most difficult feelings.

It is a bit like dropping a tincture of medicine upon our wound. We need all our attention to make sure the salve lands on just the spot.

So how do we do this?

The Practice of Kindness

We often need only add a touch of kindness, an opening of the heart to feeling our troubled feelings, in order to do the work of ending suffering.

The best way to begin this practice is to think of the phrase you wish your partner or your spouse, your best friend or your mom or dad would say to you when you are upset. It might be: "It will be alright" or "I love you just the way you are" or "Poor baby" or "It's ok" or (my favorite) a simple, sympathetic, "Ahhh".

Then when you are stuck in a structure of suffering and find it difficult to let the feelings be, speak the phrase directly to the feeling you are having trouble with, bringing your full attention to feeling the feeling as you convey kindness and compassion.

That's it.

It's a wonderful practice and you can do it all the time, with any difficult feeling. For instance, you might take the next few weeks and watch every moment for difficult feelings. Whenever you feel one, even the slightest twinge of anxiety or boredom, immediately bring kindness to it.

You might start out putting your hand on your heart or your belly and repeating your phrase until you experience clearly inside yourself what "sending kindness" feels like in your body. At that point you might be able to drop the phrase and just bring this kind feeling directly to your troubled emotion when you're caught in a structure of suffering.

> If you bring genuine kindness to yourself throughout the day, you may be astonished to discover that everyone you meet is simultaneously touched by your kindness to them.

The Warrior Scout

If not used with a delicate touch the guise of the warrior scout can
be ineffective, or even counterproductive. It is most useful when we
are really stuck, and nothing else works. It is also most effective with
depression, lethargy and confusion.

The warrior scout does not battle feelings, pushing them or blasting
them away. There is a saying that a warrior riding through enemy
territory for three days will learn as much about himself as a monk
on a three month retreat. It is this alertness in enemy territory that
the guise of the warrior scout stands for.

Not pushing the feelings of depression, lethargy or confusion away,
but like a warrior fiercely alert to every moment of sensation, never
letting ourselves get lost in stories, determined instead to meet every
moment, every articulation of transient feeling regardless of how bad
we feel, or how low we seem to be sinking. In fact, we only actually
sink when we're attaching to our thoughts and getting lost in them,
never when we're alertly watching the changing sensations of
our feelings.

It's the very place where we most want to give up or give in that
becomes our teacher. When you find yourself in this place, when
you discover that you are lost in a structure of suffering and perhaps
even despair, you should get excited and your body thrill with

energy. Right where you've been least able to find it, you call up
your vigor. At last, the moment has come. This is your opportunity
for spiritual awakening, for transformation. If you are serious about
your spiritual path this is the moment you've been waiting for all
your life. This is your edge, the boundary at which you have always
been blocked in the past. And now it has appeared one more time,
to give you another chance to burst through, to outlast the fire (it is
only a veil), to discover the transformation that comes at the end
of suffering.

Be impeccably present. Maintain fiercely your interest in each
painful moment of sensation. The pain will disappear and only
sensations and moments will remain and you will be free. But you
must be willing to be in the fire, you must have immense patience,
just watching, waiting like a cat at a mouse hole.

We are plagued by our thinking, in these difficult states. We think
that thinking will make us free. But we have much more freedom
if, by our own choice, we can be free from thinking, than we have
when we are dominated by our endless chatter. Let every thought
go. Don't pursue it a moment further. You must be persistent and
insistent with yourself. You are in the fire. If you can drop the story
there, you can drop it anywhere.

Here, the self-doubt is so strong, you need to remind yourself
constantly of your spiritual mission, of this, your greatest
opportunity. Let go of the thoughts however convincing they might
seem, and with the fierceness of a warrior, meet each moment of

sensation instead. They're not going to kill you, and even if you want to die, can't stand the pain, this is your opportunity to die to the self. When you bring your absolute attention to sensations in the body, whether feelings or the breath, you pull the plug on the self. There is no I, no me, no mine. Just dry mouth, tightness in the shoulder, agitated energy in the arms, fire in the belly. If emotional sensations become too difficult to follow, bring your attention back to the breath. Experience the breath as a lifeline through your struggle. Follow it as if your life depended on it and things will change. Right when you thought you were in the thick of it, you will find yourself free.

* * *

Meaning is not found in our ideas about things, but in the inner transformations that occur when we do things well. As you practice ending suffering using the guises of the scientist, the compassionate mother and the warrior, you will find your life suffused with meaning and filled with clarity and peace.

Greatest Teacher

I have come to experience every moment as my teacher. Small moment as much as big moment, ordinary moment as much as extraordinary, troubled moment as much as a moment of joy.

When I find myself in a mood to categorize or rank my human teachers, four of them stand out:

- My mother.
- A man who, for many years, counseled me through my greatest periods of trial.
- A spiritual teacher who died years before I was born.
- A person who made endless troubles in my life and for years made my life miserable.

It may very well be that this fourth person was my greatest teacher for it is only our worst enemy that creates the conditions for us to experience and bring to peace our rage, our humiliation, our terror, our sadness and our despair.

It is our practice of the three guises and the three ways to end suffering that brings this transformation into being. When we take on our own demons as our greatest teachers, we have begun our spiritual journey in earnest.

Working with Suffering

I can get as stuck in suffering as anyone. But the moment that I recognize I'm stuck, that I'm not working well, I get positively excited because I know I have a technique that will bring me to the end of suffering and to a transformation of its structure into something profound and meaningful.

The technique is to let thoughts go, let feelings be. It means that I must be willing to genuinely feel whatever is happening – to come inside the body and feel humiliated, for instance, rather than quickly covering it over with rage, at myself or at others.

> I have learned from this process that to feel my humiliation rather than to cover it over, deepens my humility. To feel my anger rather than act on it increases my dignity. To feel my fear rather than run from it strengthens my courage and renews my vitality.

To feel my depression rather than buy into its layers of judgment, releases me through all the suffering of living creatures into the transient nature of life itself, and into the clarity of present moments arising and the sorrow of their passing away. Through this practice I learn to both be in feelings and be at peace at the same time.

If I don't do this process I find myself locked into my habitual neurotic responses, what in the East they call karma. It is right in these places that we must wake up! Or we dig the grooves of our habits deeper and we suffer endlessly.

So, I encourage you to keep extending your range to feel all the different degrees and the different kinds of feelings you encounter. If you find yourself in a conflict, notice where in the room there is suffering. If you feel it inside yourself, immediately enter your practice. Become fearless and forgiving of your own suffering first. Over time and as you deepen your practice you may feel the suffering inside yourself just for a moment. You will then see instead that the one who has caused you harm is the only one suffering and you will be ready for the outer path of Virtue, which we will consider further in Part Two.

Cause of Suffering

You might ask, "I understand the structure of suffering, but what is its cause? How does it come about?"

The short answer is craving. Notice the next time you find yourself craving something. See if you can follow the process of craving from its inception to its conclusion. How much craving does it take for you to lose the present moment and your ability to stay steady in bodily sensations? At what point do you become filled with "I" thoughts? What other emotions besides craving do you have, and are they embedded in a structure of suffering? When do you become dominated by your feelings rather than fearless and forgiving in their midst?

Better yet, take a morning in the next week, and notice every time you crave. Whenever you do, abandon the craving, pull the plug on the self (letting go of "I" thoughts) and come back to the present moment. This is a wonderful practice to uproot the structure of suffering. You might adopt it as your primary practice for a month, for a year or for a lifetime.

Cause of Suffering:
The Three Elements

A slightly longer answer to the cause of suffering might be:

- Craving
- Aversion (craving's opposite) and
- Blanking out

In aversion we attempt to push away feelings or conditions we don't like. Most of us use aversion to push away our unpleasant feelings, even to resist the teachings in this book: "But I don't want to feel my anger, I just want to get rid of it."

Many of us also use aversion to avoid difficult situations. But in the long run aversion never works. It merely embeds states of suffering deep in our unconscious poised to arise like demons in the next crisis of our lives, keeping us ever returning frustrated and unsatisfied to structures of suffering as if they were our comfortable homes, when really they are doleful prisons locking us in illusion. We lend energy to things by not liking them. Next time you experience aversion, just notice what it is you don't like. See if you can break the aversion down into its psychic elements, into thoughts, feelings and sensations. Then let the thoughts go, let the feelings and sensations be.

All of this is not to say that there aren't times when we need to set a firm boundary, to say "No", or to act against the current of our community or our family. It is to say, rather, that the freer we are of our own suffering as we act, the clearer and more effective we will be in remedying the situation that troubles us.

Blanking out is where we lose consciousness of the present moment usually through lethargy, or attachment to self and our self-stories.

The remedy for blanking out is pulling the plug on the self and living in the present moment.

Suffering:
Cycles of Suffering

Have you ever noticed how suffering recycles itself?

One of the ways we do this is by changing our belief systems or our stories whenever suffering gets intense. Remember how suffering is just a jumble of uncomfortable feelings hooked to a series of thoughts, stories or beliefs by I, me and mine? Well, if we change our belief system, our uncomfortable feelings are likely to go away – at least for a while. Also, for a while, perhaps, the I, me or mine won't cling with such tenacity.

But before long our suffering arises again, same feelings perhaps, same I, me and mine. Just a different set of stories, that's all.

When we change our beliefs, we haven't really shifted our relationship to suffering at all. We've just recycled it.

We have a habit of clinging to thinking when we suffer. We adopted it as children so we wouldn't have to feel uncomfortable feelings. It doesn't work. The feelings keep returning.

Until we learn to find peace, to find our center amidst the chaos of common emotions, our bad habits will continue and however long we look we will fail to find the transformation that leads to the end of suffering.

Cause of Suffering:

More Cycles of Suffering

Another way that suffering keeps cycling through our lives is also driven by habit. It goes like this:

We experience a sensation from one of our six senses. (I'm including thinking as the sixth sense, each thought a mere sensation.) We have a feeling of liking, not liking or neutrality in relation to the sensation. Simply by returning to the feeling and its thoughts we foster the process of identification and attachment. We turn liking into craving, not liking into aversion and neutrality into boredom. We go further. We begin to cling to the craving and its object, the aversion and its object, or the boredom and its object with self-thoughts, creating structures of suffering.

$ in the bank
Satisfied @ Peace
> *Belief & Feeling*

Envy as stock market
soars
> *New Feeling*

Puts $ in market
> *New Belief & Action*

The end result of clinging is always suffering. We fall into darkness, blanking out. The next thing we are aware of is another sensation to which we respond with a feeling of liking, not liking or neutrality. Not knowing any other way, we pursue this sensation as well into craving and clinging and suffering. And so the world turns.

We respond to sensations out of habit, but it is the sensations that give us our one opportunity for freedom from this cycle of suffering. If when we felt a sensation, instead of being pulled by our habitual emotional responses, we simply felt the sensation, and living in the present moment nimbly shifted our awareness to the next sensation and so on, we would find freedom from suffering instead.

Market crashes
> *New Suffering*

Poverty is blessed
> *New Belief*

Crisis: leak in
roof & no $
> *New Suffering*

The Habit of Suffering

Craving - In town:

1. 1st thought of Ice Cream
> *Sensation*

2. Smiling
> *Liking*

3. Elaborating, returning to thought
> *Craving*

Aversion - At a dinner party: Broccoli

1. 1st smell of broccoli
> *Sensation*

2. Frowning
> *Not Liking*

3. Returning to image of discomfort re: broccoli
> *Aversion*

4. Going to get ice cream, blinders on – black raspberry Baskin Robbins
> *Clinging*

5. Full, fat bloated suffering
> *Becoming/Suffering/ Blanking out*

4."How could she?" Going over all the vegetables the hostess could have served instead and all your excuses for not eating.
> *Clinging to Aversion*

5. Totally lost to everyone at party. Unhappy, tense, angry
> *Becoming/Suffering/ Blanking out*

Boredom - Going to visit Uncle Bob. You're not really interested:

1. 1st Thought of
Uncle Bob
> *Sensation*

2. Neutral expression
> *Neutrality*

3. Returning to image of
not being interested.
> *Boredom*

The Gang of Five

Sometimes suffering arises not from a single source, but from
multiple sources all at once. The most common example of this is
what I call "The Gang of Five." Here both craving and aversion hit
us at the same time. And blanking out hits us as well wearing the
masks of lethargy, restlessness and doubt.

Virtually any uncomfortable situation can set off the gang of five: a
sudden visit by a bill collector, a cancelled plane, disappointment in love
or on the job, or a health concern. Even trying to meditate can set off the
gang. Let's see how:

4. Playing out all the other things you could be doing and all the ways Bob is boring.
> *Clinging to Boredom*

5. With Bob, but totally lost in fantasy, dulled out, desperately trying to avoid the tedium of each moment.
> *Becoming/Suffering/ Blanking out*

As I sit down to meditate I keep thinking (restlessness): "I don't want to do this" (aversion), "I'd rather take a walk" (craving) "in fact, I don't think I'll be any good at meditating today, because I'd rather do something else" (doubt) and then because I'm being pulled by so many forces away from the present moment I have trouble finding the breath and may just get sleepy instead (lethargy).

The problem with an attack by the gang of five is that, if you focus with meditative skill on any one of them with any degree of success (say craving or lethargy), the other four will come at you all the more strongly. It's rather like getting caught in fly paper. Just when you think one part of your body is getting free, three other parts are getting stuck.

The remedy for an attack by the gang of five is not to do what we've been doing: breaking down suffering into its elements. You will find yourself attacked all the more fiercely by the elements you've left out. Rather, each time any one of the five disturbs you, recognize that it is the whole gang that's plaguing you, not just one element. Remind yourself that they have no substance individually, transforming themselves into each other as they do. Determine not to respond to any of them, when they attack, simply label them in the moment, "the gang of five" and return to the breath (or sensations) as a way to live in the present moment. Do this repeatedly. Be persistent.

Notice that the messages of the gang are "I-messages" and, when you return to the present moment, you pull the plug on the self.

Facing their blustery storm, you will know what it is to be fearless and forgiving in the midst of suffering.

Our Obsessive Loops

Did you ever notice when you're really upset how you go through one story after another of your struggle only to arrive back at the story that you started it all with – and then you repeat each of the stories again? And again and again. This is another way that a cycle of suffering keeps going. Let's see how it works.

Look first at all the different structures of suffering that come up around a traumatic event. Sometimes they are all driven by (or driving) the same emotion, although more often there are subtle differences. Look at each story you tell yourself, look at the feeling that underlies it and at the I, me and mine that holds it together. Then look at what other troubling feeling is missing, emotionally, in each story. Usually, the missing or underplayed emotion in a particular story will be the predominant emotion in the very next story of your obsessive loop.

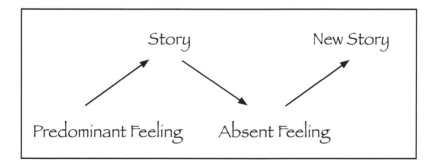

So, for instance, you're driving home from work replaying a fight you just had with your boss. The structure of your suffering is anger (*uncomfortable feeling*) hooked to your ***thoughts and stories*** of the incident by your process of ***identification*** ("*I'm* so angry at you" or "How dare he do that to *me*").

Before long a *feeling of terror* arises as you realize your anger was over the top. Your ***story and identification*** are established with the thought "*I* might lose *my* job".

As you play that story out a *feeling of guilt* begins to arise which gets hooked to the ***thought*** "What have *I* done?" by another process of ***identification***.

And then ***humiliation*** arises which gets attached to a ***story*** of an apology and flowers by your ***identifying*** which leads to a *feeling of despair* attached to the story and ***identity*** of "*I* won't ever get what *I* need at this job."

Of course your next *feeling is frustration* which leads you to reason with your boss as you did at the beginning of the fight, and "*I* am being perfectly reasonable" is the ***thought of identification.***

Your next feeling is anger which leads you right back to the fight where the whole obsessive process began.

Whichever you experience coming first, a thought or a feeling, they do a dance together, leading into each other. A feeling leads to a story which leads to another feeling which leads to a thought. Like the dial on the face of a clock, we go around till we return to the same set of stories all over again.

If you do the work of the third intention, being fearless and forgiving in the midst of suffering, you will learn to be comfortable with your feelings. They won't attach so easily to your thoughts and stories. If you keep your focus on the emotional experience of a process, letting your thoughts go, you will soon feel your way through these situations as if you were following a golden thread of holy spirit rather than a logic-chopping analysis that keeps hooking you back to structures of suffering and to *me*. The three intentions are a more efficient way of processing suffering than thinking and analyzing—a much deeper way, a way that leads to wisdom rather than keeping you in terror.

When you find yourself suffering, learn to watch the thousand nuances of emotion and changing sensations rippling through the body. Keep present in each moment. Let your thoughts go.

At the end of a process of feeling, which may last from two minutes to two hours, you've usually arrived at the truth of a situation, at an inner peace, and an understanding of what you must do if you need to do anything at all.

Entering the Fire

Blake, Dante, Jesus, Buddha, Odysseus, Rumi, Rama, Daniel. What did they have in common besides being teachers to us all? They each entered the fire, faced their demons or wandered through hell as part of their spiritual journey. They chose to do this, and it was their choice that made them great and that inspires each of us caught in our own flames, to do likewise. Without facing their fire they would never have become whom we all respect them as being. Heroes, spiritual figures, saviors.

We think of certain figures in our lifetime as having gone through similar periods of trial. Ghandi and Nelson Mandela come to mind.

What we miss by romanticizing these journeys of others is the depth and passion and profundity of our own similar journeys.

What happens when we discover a horrible secret, when we are betrayed by others, when our marriage hangs on by a thread, or our child dies? What happens when we get caught up in a scandal where we meant no harm (or perhaps just a little harm) or we lose our job and our home? What is it like when it feels our life's purpose slips endlessly out of our grip, or disease ravages our body, or the world about us is consumed in war? What happens when someone rapes us or beats us?

And on a more mundane level, daily, what happens when you don't get to the post office on time, when your washing machine breaks down or you have a flat tire? What happens when you come home to 350 emails, when you discover a rash all over your body, or your boss berates you, or your partner leaves your house a mess, or you find out your son has been skipping school? What is it like for you when you wake up and face the day with dread or with weariness or with grief?

Are these not our demons, our infernos and our fires? Are these not exactly the places where we also face the choice of building structures of suffering that will entrap us, or entering our fire?

Plunge into the fire! Be fearless. Don't diminish your life, or rob it of meaning. What is the demon in your difficult situation? What is the fire? Do you feel it in your face? Does it burn you from your thighs to the furrows on your brow? Does it set you all atremble?

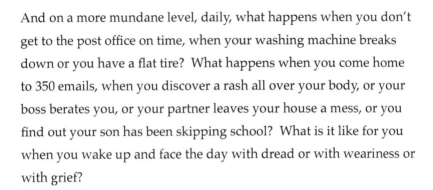

This is the work and the practice of suffering. Without this, there is no release. Find what is true, what is deep and what is on fire. It will be in your senses, not in your stories. Let your body come alive in the flames.

It's like a cyclone. Feel the strength that comes from living in its midst. Find the eye of the storm, the eye that observes each sensation as it arises, the eye that feels every feeling, letting the thoughts go. The eye is calm. The storm is felt and moves on.

On some level, and the most profound, what you are going through has nothing to do with "them" or "it," and nothing to do with your stories of yourself. On the level where your experience is universal and universally true, what you're going through is, as feelings are, beyond words. This is the level on which life must be experienced if we are to achieve the rite of passage from that which troubles the world to that which releases it into freedom.

The End of Suffering

*"Only those who have truly suffered know what
it is to transform the fires and torments of hell into
the tears and fountains of heaven."*

Anonymous

There is an end to suffering that we experience as absolute and irrevocable. As quick as a lightening bolt, as light as a feather, timeless, it arises in a moment and while seeming to pass away in the very next, stays like the ripples of warmth on a late spring day. It changes everything and everything stays the same.

Suffering's wisdom is not a plateau we arrive at. Living the truth is not a static state, but an ongoing rite of passage like winter

blustering into spring. What is revealed in the ending of suffering is just that, the ending of suffering—exactly how it occurs, how suffering arises (or begins to arise) and how we bring it to peace, universally, inside ourselves so that we might pass the peace to others. It is something nourishing like breathing that, once we've learned, we relish practicing until we die.

Life is here to be lived. What the three intentions do, is give us a process by which we might experience each moment of life's arising, unblocked by either analysis or by clinging—neither by the world out there nor by the ego's appropriation of the world in here.

Life itself is onrushing. Blake calls it fountains of living waters. Countless mystics, including Blake, talk of entering the fire. Suffering's wisdom is achieved in the experience of these fires and waters rushing through our demonic caverns and the darkest recesses of our brains into our most fertile soil and the flowering branches of paradise. Through the experience of understanding, of letting thoughts go and feelings be, we come to realize that each of our nightmares has been meant as a rite of passage to wake us into life itself—not merely from the nightmare, but truly into life.

Without the forgiveness that gives us the strength to be with the darkest of our feelings, life does not come into being. With it, everything becomes human. On the other side of the objects we experience, which inevitably place limits on our vision and all our senses, is life itself. Living in the present moment, letting the opaque self go, the inner world is not blocked by objects. Listen to its music which never stops, follow its thread and you will discover that the string it plays upon is life itself, and a human life, at that.

No Inside, No Outside

It takes work to experience transformation, to come to the place where the ending of suffering is second nature to us and we are ready for what's next.

Along the way, there are markers. Like the time we go out of our way to do a good deed, and it doesn't come across. The person we were doing it for wasn't there, or didn't appreciate it. And instead of or in spite of or even in the midst of feeling disappointed or shamed, we experience light breaking through all the surfaces of our body and a feeling of joy that seems to lift us up out of the top third of our spine into the very air itself. And we know that outcomes don't matter, that virtue is its own reward, that what changes changes in here as much as out there, and that the change is forever.

Or like when we find our emotions in our bodies for the very first time, and it feels so awful, we feel like we've gone backwards, and want to throw up. But within weeks we recognize a whole world we'd never seen before. Something has connected us to waving plants and to trees and to the ripples of the landscape they are in, and to the depths of despair or delight in the palpitations of a crease along the corner of a stranger's mouth. We feel it in our gut and recognize we've gone deeper than we've ever gone before.

Or when we recognize with a thrill that the difficult things that happen to us, only happen to make us better people, and are opportunities calling out to us to test our powers of transformation.

The fundamental marker that each of these reflects is a turning about in the seat of consciousness that shifts our experience from an outward grasping of thoughts and circumstances to an inward experiencing of moments transforming. Deep within that "turning about" lie the three ways to end suffering and our intimate understanding that it is to them and to the ending of suffering itself that all of our life is dedicated.

What happens next is the hard work of the practice of ending suffering that we must repeat for years until the experience of confronting our neuroses, of breaking habits and ending karma becomes so clear to us that the ending of suffering is internalized as the process of life itself, as something that happens every day.

We see that there is no inside, no outside to our experience, and it is time to go forth. Our inauthentic selves have been accepted. Our dark, unruly feelings have been embraced. As we feel a renewed energy and vitality coursing through our bodies, we call upon all the forces of nature to support us moving out into the world, because they are part of ourselves. It is said that an electron jumping orbits at the other end of our galaxy conveys enough energy to this earth to impact a game of pool. How much more powerful and far-reaching than anything we know must be our acts of kindness to one another.

If you are serious about ending suffering, do this three-fold practice and you will end it, both inside yourself and in the world. Pull the plug on the self, live in the present moment and be fearless and forgiving in the midst of suffering.

Wherever you see suffering you will know how to transform it. Your impact on the world will be like the nourishment of the sun's shining light on all living creatures. Like rain. Like the earth itself.

We become the secret spies of God, secret angels in goodness and delight, and her secret demons, experiencing richly even our demonic natures and in the very richness of our experience, transforming them into what is true, what is beautiful, what is on fire, what is fresh and what is alive.

Part Two

The Outer Pathway:
Awaking to the Pathway

For days, on retreat, I have felt exhilarated from practicing the three intentions. This afternoon as part of my practice I have been walking back and forth across a wide room. For hours I have felt alive and present except that every time my bare foot comes down, heel first on the cool surface of the wood floor I blank out. I go unconscious, I can't find the moment. So I've been looking very carefully, trying to sneak up on it, watching what happens just before, as my foot is falling to the floor, and just after, as I experience a coolness in the heel moving toward the outer edge of my foot as it makes contact with the floor. But nothing works! I go faster. I go slower. It doesn't work. Finally frustrated but inspired, lonely and longing but alive to the challenge, I think of my 'Circle of Angels', a group of inspiring beings I look to for wisdom when times get tough. They include Saint Francis, the Dalai Lama, a personal mentor, a member of my family, Mother Teresa and a few others. I think, "I'll just ask them!" My gaze stays on the floor in front of me, my hands held humbly at my waist, but with an inner gaze I look up, and with an inner gesture reach up, arms held open to the sky. And I experience their kindly and compassionate eyes looking down at me. Suddenly my falling foot is alive with sensations of the floor and a rushing river of energies rises through my body and soars out

*the top of my head, opening into a circle like rays of magnetism releasing,
rushing through my body out into a shower of energy above me. I am
stunned, having only experienced this kind of sensation in my dreams. I
have no idea how long I stand there, but within a few minutes I think to
myself, "I am letting all this energy go. Why not bring it back inside me?"
And very gently I direct the energy back, like rays of magnetism, stretching
out above me and then downward in front of me and then coalescing back
into my body just below my navel. And so this river of energy runs in
circles around and through me, and I feel bathed by light and energy, and
for the first time in my life, present in every moment.*

*Soon thereafter, I find myself sitting in meditation in an entirely new way.
Daring, loose and at ease with moments, I have shifted from following my
breath at the nostrils to my belly. Present, but relaxed and spacious with
my awareness, I allow the breath to show or not show, or to half reveal itself
between the most subtle of sensations. For me it is like the time I really
learned to ride a horse, where there was no difference between me and the
horse, except for the subtlest shifts of attention and direction that I gave.*

*I begin to walk with a similar looseness. Walking with presence, ease
– a flow within all the transitory moments clicking on and off, aware of
everything, but as gracious with absences as with presences. And suddenly
in the middle of that ease and that alertness, everything stops. My walking
stops, the world stops, there is no 'I' here. I really can't describe it. I
have no idea how long it lasts, but my guess is less than a second. I just
know, after that moment, that everything has shifted. It is as if I have been
reorganized – not my mind so much as my whole being. I stand there,
afterward, not wanting to move, but wanting to give as much space as*

*possible for whatever has happened to mature, to flourish in its own way. I
stand for close to two hours, experiencing stillness and the silence within
the songs and the soft breezes of spring. I am stunned, still, enthralled,
happy, and at ease. Slowly I begin to move, and then go on with my day as
if nothing has changed, take a walk, have dinner, go to bed. But in bed, at
night, I can't turn the light out, the one inside me that brings the soft covers
and sweet chalky greyness of sleep. I am wide awake like never before, eyes
closed, a blazing light shining all around and inside me. It is as if my body
is a light bulb. Throughout this experience I feel confident that I am free
of all the work I've ever done, free of the past and the future, free of all the
teachings I have given. What comes to me with a certainty that feels like
thunder, is an understanding of the three intentions and of the pathway to
realize them in the world.*

Entering the World

So how do I take this wonderful world, this deep world, this challenging world, this world inside me that transforms suffering into wisdom – how do I take this world out into everything I do? Into my relationships, into my sleep, into my work, into the seemingly endless repetitive details of my life, so that each and every one of those places becomes a place of rest, a place of dedication and focus, of nimbleness and ease – a place of practice, where even there, everywhere, is the possibility of transformation and wisdom.

For if now I experience those places as mundane, troubling or boring, aren't I missing completely the three intentions to "Live in the Present Moment, Pull the Plug on the Self, and Be Fearless and Forgiving in the Midst of Suffering," and their fruit, which is the transformation of suffering into wisdom?

What if we were to build up a world inside of us, where in this way each place we pause to do the work becomes a place of wisdom? And since the places where we pause to do this work are seemingly outside of us, "in the world", what would that world be like, what would it then become?

Let's take a survey of all of those places in our lives today, and begin our work!

Daily Habits and Ordinary Events

W e start our "outer path" with the three intentions and the ordinary events of our daily lives.

Let's begin by taking a single activity that we do every day. It could be anything—driving your car, taking a shower, brushing your teeth, putting on clothes, opening the mail, opening doors, eating, going to the bathroom, talking on the telephone, surfing the web—really anything could do.

Take transportation as an example, how you get from here to there. How can you make your experience of that into a spiritual path – a path of presence? Of course if you use public transportation you could always just do inner listening, closed-eyed and focused on the breath. Or you could do an open-eyed meditation, bringing in the hustle and the bustle, incorporating sounds and smells as well, being present with it all. But what about driving? How do you make driving into a practice without becoming a danger on the roads? How do you make something practical part of your path to suffering's wisdom?

> Just by paying attention.

So, next time you get in your car, pause for a moment. Notice the sensations of just sitting there. Notice how the seat feels against your back, your hips and your thighs. Notice your breath. Notice how your hands feel on the steering wheel. Are they clammy or dry, clenched or at ease? Notice how the wheel feels. Does it feel hard or soft, warm or cool? These are all places to return to, much like the breath in a closed-eyed meditation. Of course your overriding intention is to be fully alert to the task of driving—to both safety and to getting you where you want to go.

So, having made the commitment to safety and "getting there", instead of wandering off into your favorite preoccupations and daydreams or into curses at being late or at so much to do, bring a nimble awareness to all the changing sensations you experience. Notice sensations in the body, notice the sounds of the motor, of the tires or of the cars going by or the wind or the rain. Notice your breath. Notice, without stories, just bare sensations, all the changes to what you are seeing and sensing.

Suddenly, what was a trip to the drug store that you viewed as boring or repetitive, has become quite interesting, fresh and alive. And whereas you might otherwise have become lost in a story about your daughter's sixth grade teacher, or your need for a new cell phone, or about what might be awaiting you when you finish at the drugstore and pickup your mail at the post office, instead, intermittent with these thoughts (which you let go of) every moment is alive, sparkling with light or moisture's condensation and with the movement of the breath in the belly, the bushes by the road, the sudden horn of a neighbor's car blaring and fading, now far away from you. The momentary thought of a betrayal might plunge you into the irreproachable darkness of despair or a heaviness in the belly, as you wave to the neighbor you're passing by and turn right on red with fragile feelings crawling like spiders from your fingers up your arms to your throat. Pulling into the parking lot, you lift your foot and feel the solid downward pressure of the brake, feel the

car door as it opens and shuts and inside, walking down the aisles, hearing a subtle crispness in the air itself break against the Beatles "She loves you", you feel a pulsing into your shoulders and notice a moment of shame as you reach for a Reese's Cup and add it to your pile of toothpaste, aspirin and shampoo bringing your practice right into the drugstore with you. And then the person behind the counter—you see nothing but kindness in them and give nothing but kindness to them. The colors in the store rushing by you as you move, the contrast of the air-conditioned air, walking one step after another out the doors unfolding into moisture and light.

Every daily activity is filled with passion and light, if we will only bring our attention to it. Take just one activity a month, and see what happens when, each time you do it, you bring the four qualities and the three intentions to it.

One Day a Month

Sometimes doing a daily meditation practice along with an
occasional practice of noticing daily activities just isn't enough.
Nothing seems to be happening. Nothing changes.

My prescription?

Take one day a month—that's 12 days a year—and lock your five
sense doors out of everything but NOW – for each moment of
that day, choose what you want to do. Make living in the present
moment your total dedication.

It's like this: if you want to do a laundry, start the laundry, but if
you get to the point of putting the soap in and right at that moment
you don't want to put the soap in, you want to smell the outdoor
air, well forget about the laundry, walk to the window or the door,
feeling every arm swing and foot fall as you go, and let the air fill
your nostrils with its freshness. Smell the air. Take its temperature at
the surface of your skin, let its moisture or its dryness wash through
you. If you feel like reading a book, you must choose in each
moment to continue reading and at the first inkling you no longer
want to read, you drop the book, you don't finish the chapter, you
don't finish the paragraph, you don't even finish the sentence, but
you move right on to what calls you next. For a whole day a month,
live only in moments of your own choosing. Remember, if in your

quietest inner listening you find five moments in a second, then practice with the intention of living freshly 300 moments a minute, 18,000 moments an hour. Each one chosen freshly, each authentically yours.

So get your calendar out. Find a day this month that works for you and draw an X across it. Better yet, draw a big banner at the top of the page and put "MY DAY" in it, or "Day of Presence" "Day of Wonder" or "Day of Delight" or whatever makes your heart sing. Put a splash of color into it.

Then do the same for a day in each of the months that follow.

Taking a Walk

Walking is a wonderful time to practice living in the present moment. Whether you're walking outside in the country, along a windy beach, through the halls of work, or on a busy city street,

> Live in your senses.

Let your thoughts go. It can be thrilling to walk in nature for an hour, listening to every sound, feeling the wind on your torso and the movement of your limbs, alive to every changing fragrance on the breeze, and letting all your thoughts go. You can do this in an office setting as well. Though it may not seem as adventurous or romantic, it can bring freshness and ease to a stress-filled day—even when the smells are of toner and coffee, and the sounds are the hum and whrrr of machines or the chatter of people.

City Walks

For years I did a walking practice as a daily meditation through
the busy city streets of Harvard Square. Early on I realized a few
obstacles to my practice of living in the present moment. If my gaze

wandered through shop windows, I might find my mind wandering into mazes of desire. If I heard a fragment of a conversation I could find myself filling in all its details. And if I found myself looking at a person's face, I would immediately form a liking or disliking of them

and create a story of my relationship to them that would be filled with aversion or with desire.

So I changed my practice.

> I restricted my sense of sight to the sidewalk a few feet in front of me, and became fierce with my sense of sound. I would let all sounds in except for words. If there were many words around, I would focus exclusively on sight and physical sensation.

Back in those days I knew many people in Cambridge. I don't think any of them knew what I was doing, when they would greet me with "George!" I would look up, cry out "Richard! How are you?" exchange a few sentences of amusement, commiseration or delight, and return my gaze to the ground and my practice to sensing.

It's not a dangerous practice, although watch out at street corners! Allow your gaze to look both ways. I did this practice daily for fifteen years, and only once in all those years did I walk into a lamppost.

Nighttime Practice

There are two practices of the nighttime. In one we fill the wakeful moments of our nights with presence. In the other we bring the four qualities of *dedication, focus, agility* and *balance* right into our dreams, so that we are aware that we are dreaming as we dream—fully awake within them.

It is best, in your early days of practice, to choose one of the nighttime practices and attain some mastery of it before picking up the other one. Their instructions conflict a bit as to what to do with the wakeful moments of your night. Once you've had some success with both, you will find it easier to weave your nighttime practice from these two separate threads.

Being Present in Darkness

The more comprehensive of the two practices of the nighttime, is
to bring presence into all your wakeful moments. Paradoxically,
it's a wonderful cure for insomnia. Let's say you frequently find
yourself awake in the middle of the night, unable to return to sleep.
You've tried many things. You've turned on the light and read.
You've gotten up and gone to the kitchen for some tea or a piece of
cake. But most of all it seems you have tossed and turned, as if you
were pages in a suspense novel, frustrated and cursing at each turn,
desperately trying to get back to sleep.

Instead try this. Stop trying to get back to sleep, but don't get up,
don't turn on the light, don't get something to eat. Open your eyes
for a while and marvel at what an extraordinary experience it is
to touch the night in all its qualities. Notice how visually you can
almost feel the darkness in its broken shades of gray. Notice how
the air feels on your skin, how the sheets softly sweep across your
belly as it rises and falls. Notice the sounds of the wind, of the
radiator, of the cars swishing by, of your partner's breath. Notice
the stillness in which your own breath rests. As you notice these
things keep returning to bare sensations, stripped of stories and
common meanings. See the darkness with a fresh eye for just form
and tone. Hear the sounds of the night just as pitch, timbre, volume
and rhythm. Feel the sensations of lying in darkness. Feel them
from the tip of your toes to the top of your head—the transience

of temperature, movement, location and shape. Return to the sensations of breathing. Rest in its rhythm. And as you relax into the nighttime, let your eyes close and continue your observation and appreciation of the unending sea of sensations and sound.

If you are not subject to insomnia, the only difference in the instructions is not to open your eyes, but every time you wake up, and even as you first go to bed, bring your awareness to the whole ocean of sensations you experience. At last focusing on the breath itself, without a narrow focus, just rest in the rhythm of the breath. Allow the sensation of the belly's rise and fall and of the sheets and nightclothes to be part of your experience.

Waking Up Inside Your Dreams

When I meet people who are plagued with nightmares I surprise
them by telling them how lucky they are. "Your nightmares, they are
gifts from God," I tell them.

There is a moment in a nightmare when we know we are dreaming.
That moment happens rarely in other dreams, and far too rarely in
our waking life, but it happens once in every nightmare. It's the
moment when we say to ourselves "I've got to wake up. I'm in a
nightmare." If only we knew what a very special moment that is.
We don't give it a second thought. We are filled with aversion, seek
desperately to escape the dream world, and so wake up—usually
to fearful chills and shaking, so disturbing has the dream been. We
have woken up from a nightmare, not genuinely to end it, but to
keep it going emotionally and psychologically inside us, sometimes
for hours after.

The trick is to wake up in the dream, not from the dream.

> If only we were so lucky in our waking life to realize we
> are dreaming and to wake up inside this dream, perhaps
> paradise or enlightenment would not be so far away from
> this chilly earth.

I first learned this practice in my 20's, when I had nightmares almost every night, frequently several in a night, the world seemed that threatening to me. I remember one night being chased by some awful spirit, some darkness in the nighttime that I never fully saw. Running wildly with all speed over the hills I came to a tower that I thought meant safety, went inside and began to climb its spiral staircase. Halfway up I realized there was no exit. I was trapped.

Suddenly I realized, "I'm in a nightmare. I can wake up from this dream." And then I realized that if it was just a dream, I could do anything I wanted, the dark spectre that was chasing me was not real, or at best a metaphor; it could have no hold on me. I decided to experiment. Still, shaken in the moment by the terror that had preceded, I wondered "What is it that I need in this moment?"

I realized I needed to be more connected with who I was, so I just looked down, gazed into the palms of my hands and felt this rush of human feeling pour through me till its warmth seemed to melt the wall around me, and its power carried me soaring into the nighttime sky.

The intermingling of self-knowing and freedom that I experienced in that dream filled me with determination to do it again. The next night gave me that opportunity. This time I was being chased by an ogre and had tripped on a branch.

Looking up at the figure towering over me with his sword raised over his head, I became aware once again that I was dreaming. Once

again I knew that I could choose to do anything in the dream or to wake myself up from it. "What if I just let him chop my head off?" I wondered as his sword came at me. And as my head rolled away from my body I experienced my spirit come out of my neck and fly once again into the sky, filled with power and with awe.

The next night another giant chased me, only this time I decided to befriend it. "Take me to your leader," I said. Its angry and terrifying expression turned into a sheepish grin as it led me on a marvelous adventure through forests and bogs and caves to the world of the giants.

Each morning, after these dreams, I would awake to the realization that the particular daytime anxieties and fears that had given rise to the prior night's dream, had been dispelled. Rushes of power, vitality and self-confidence began to replace my experience of the threatening world outside. As good as any therapy, I thought, or great friendship, is to learn to be our own best friend and to wake up inside our dreams.

Since that time, there have been many wonders, waking inside my dreams, profound spiritual experiences and great rushes of creativity. But soon enough, the nightmare's gift from God receded from my everyday experience as my anxieties diminished. I had to teach myself instead another way of waking inside my dreams. While it has many permutations, the core of it is simple. It goes like this.

As I'm going to sleep, and whenever I wake in the night, I remind myself, "Next time I'm dreaming I want to be aware I'm dreaming." I keep reminding myself as I fall back asleep so that it's the last thing I'm aware of in my conscious mind. For me, it works almost every time. For others, whom I've taught, it can take a week or two to experience the first lucid dream.

Stephen LaBerge describes a similar technique in his books on lucid dreaming. There have been many books written on the topic. I recommend them.

In Sickness

When you've just begun this practice, and you get a cold, or the flu, you think "I can't meditate because I'm sick." In fact, when we are sick we may not be able to go to work or to shop or take care of others or exercise or visit friends. But the one thing we can do, even twenty-four hours a day, if we want to, is meditate.

"But my nose is stuffed up, I can't breath." Funny, I haven't met anyone yet who's said this who wasn't actually breathing. If you can't follow the breath at the nostrils, switch to the belly or to the mouth. Or if you're lying in bed, feverish, and feeling all achy, bring your meditation to all the changing sensations in your body. Even better, bring kindness and compassion to each of these troubled sensations, letting your structures of suffering go. What they really want is comfort and bringing kindness to every feeling. Your bedside manner moment by moment throughout the day and night is far better than a doctor's in a five minute office visit.

"But I'm so tired I keep falling asleep." So do your nighttime practice of moving back and forth between meditation and sleep, always steady in one or the other, always bringing care and comfort to your most uncomfortable feelings.

The sea of sensations in the body will become as calming as the ocean itself, as comforting as the random sounds of the radiator conveying the morning heat, or the sounds of cars swishing by on a rainy morning. Like leaves rustling in the wind, or the pattern that rain drops make on our window there is the wisdom of life itself in the multitudinous sensations of the body resting in the wakeful moments of the night.

> This healing wisdom when we are sick or troubled reaches down into the center of our being and brings spiritual medicine back and spreads it into every corner of our body.

Pay attention. Don't miss a moment or a sensation, and as you let go of the conceptual world, all of your troubles will pass away from you as well.

Since I've learned this practice, most of my flus and colds have lasted a fraction of the time they used to. Even more important, I enjoy every minute. It's as if I'm resting in the lap of God, having given over myself utterly and in misery to spiritual practice. "How do misery and enjoyment go together?" you ask. There's no me to the misery, just its passion and its music.

Moderation

<u>Nourishment</u>

It is indeed surprisingly difficult to live a life of moderation. In a world filled with so much pleasure and so many enticements, it is easy to feel that if we abstain, we are being deprived. I think of abstinence in a different way. I think of abstinence as being like meditation. I think of it as developing an inner calm in the midst of suffering. A quiet abstinence, where we let our thoughts go and feel our feelings, has profound depth. Abstinence calls upon us to find genuine pleasure inside and from inward actions rather than from things we acquire in the world. It develops fortitude. It cultivates the virtue of patience. To be dependent on the external world for our pleasures only leads to suffering.

As we do the work of the three intentions, we find that what is healthiest for us actually brings us the most pleasure.

<u>Food</u>

Most of us are overweight. Many of those who are not, are hugely concerned about the relationship of their weight to their appearance. We pay little more than lip-service to the profound studies linking our diets to our lifespan. By dying early, in the service of our tongues, we throw away years of potential wisdom-giving that is the birthright and aim of becoming elders in our communities, of growing old. We've known for many years that a highly nutritious diet of 30%

less calories than average will lead to both considerably longer and considerably healthier lives. The studies are quite clear. If you want to live several decades longer, to slow all the processes of aging and to live freer of disease and disability as you age, eat less – a little hunger is a good thing, if your diet is balanced and nutritious.

Drink & Drugs

Why do we consume so many things that take us up or bring us down? Do they help us to be fearless and forgiving in the midst of suffering or do they remove us a step or two from our natural pace of feeling? Do they help us to clearly and consistently pull the plug on the self or do they increase selfing or obscure it? Do they help us live freshly in the present moment or do they merely speed us up or slow us down and thus put a veil across our natural rhythm? Do they nourish the body leading to a longer and healthier life? Do they develop powers within our chaotic and troubled minds, our inner natures and capacities, or do they cede those powers to other influences? What do you think? Is it better to use moderation in drink and drugs? Is it best not to use them at all?

Money

Live well within your means. I've spent most of my professional life working in the world of money, and those who are most at peace around money live this way. Saving is a form of abstinence. All of our suffering, all our confusion and cursing, all the ways we're stuck in ambivalences come from our desires being larger than our capacities or our accomplishments. To act upon these desires in the realm of money bankrupts us, and bankrupts the meaning in our

lives as well. If you feel your money life is more complex or fraught than this, seek out someone with training or certification as a Life Planner, someone trained to marry the meaning and money in your life. There is no reason not to live in balance both with the forces of money and the forces of meaning in your life.

Time
A Simple Life

There are days where I feel run by the complexities of my life. And there are other, quite wonderful days where every choice I make is toward simplicity. One thing at a time. Staying near the senses. Not pushing. Never multi-tasking. At one with the wind or the sounds of the birds and with my actions, my body and my breath.

We wear our lives' details like layers of cloth to hide from ourselves and others both our simplicity and our nakedness.

Most everyone I know longs for a simpler life. A simpler life doesn't necessarily mean giving away your possessions, although it might. A simple life will be quite different from person to person. Some might bring all their misery with them into their new, outwardly simple, life. Some might be rich, some might be poor.

Most of us think of the simple life as being a life free of daily demands and responsibilities, and often free of things. This is the most straightforward way to simplify. Sometimes, if we look at people we think live simple lives, we discover they're just as busy as we are. In their movement toward simplicity, what they've given up primarily is their attachment to themselves, and to how they are perceived in the world. They've stopped projecting their search for inner wealth onto the outer world. When we hang out around them, we don't perceive their attachment to the things of this world, and that helps us feel peaceful as well.

For those of us who can't manage the simple life, it is most often the emotional exposure we can't yet bear. We can only live a simple life if we are willing to be more of who we are, because that is what remains when all the complexity of life falls away.

Look at your own life. Take some time to pause and reflect. Keep returning to this place until you find the answer. What do you need to do to live a simple life?

Work-Life Balance

A useful way we frame our yearning for a simple life is "Work-Life Balance". Do we have a good balance between work and the rest of our life, or do we work so hard we have no time for ourselves, or for our family? Does our cell phone follow us on vacation, or on family time? Are we doing email into the endless hours of evening?

Perhaps for a few of us this is a lifestyle in which we can flourish. But for most of us, we need to ask the question "Who am I living for?" "Does my life feel comfortable and at ease, or am I constantly stressed out and rushing about?"

Not nearly often enough do we take action when we ask ourselves, "Do I need to live more simply?" and "What would life be like if I earned less and spent less?" Too seldom we ask ourselves, " How can I maximize the time I live in the present moment?" or "How can I maximize my inner wealth, as opposed to my outer wealth?"

Relationships

Our relationships with others often contain the key both to a simple life, and to transforming our suffering into wisdom.

Living in community, relationship or family, most of us fall into patterns of wanting or pleasing. What would be the way of harmony, simple and selfless instead? Is it possible to hone close to the three intentions, and to practice acts of kindness without hooks to ourselves or to others?

First, you must consider who is your community.

There is nothing more wonderful than sharing your journey with others or with another, and, nothing more devastating than sharing your life with those actively hostile to the inner work you are doing.

Seek out friends who support you. Work with your spouse or your partner so that they understand what you're doing. See if you can inspire each other, play off each other – whether by meditating together, or wrestling with the same ethical dilemmas, or best of all, sharing the dedicated practices of simple human kindness and support.

Couples and Friends
In Conflict

When we are in conflict with our partners, best to practice being
fearless and forgiving. Recognizing that we are on an inward
journey and that it's more about us than it is about them can help to
bring a quicker resolution to our struggles. It will also foster much
more dramatic personal growth for us in the process.

> Let your thoughts go. Let your feelings be. Rest in the
> random chaos of sensations and feelings, the ocean of
> emotion and sense that is the ground of your being.

Find your way to at least an inkling of suffering's wisdom before you
even begin to speak.

And when you do speak, connect with your partner around feelings
first. Don't try to "solve the problem" or "explain" what's really
happening. That will only cause attachment to your own thoughts,
while your partner develops an equal measure of aversion.

Try first to completely identify with how your partner must
be *feeling*. You may disagree with their thinking, but you can
nonetheless understand how they feel, given their thinking. Let
them know how sorry you are that anything you might do or have

done could cause them so much pain. Let them know that if you were them, and were thinking along their lines that you would feel just as angry, just as disappointed, just as upset as they are. Let them really hear this before you go any further. Make sure they really feel your empathy, or you will not be able to go any further. There is a magic to this work for your relationships. Suffering's wisdom saves marriages and maintains long-lasting friendships.

Once your partner has heard you and there is a genuine softening in the tone of your conversation, then you can share your feelings. Tentatively, at first—careful not to press their buttons—and not your "thinking", not your "explanation" but rather how anxious you have felt, fearful, disappointed and angry yourself. And how much you don't want to be stuck in that place together with your partner. If you're lucky (or with a bit of training) your partner will empathize with you, the tone will be softer still, and possibly then, or a short time thereafter you will be able to discuss the facts of your difference and how the two of you want to go forward.

Couples and Friends: Forgiveness

Forgiveness is often the key. Particularly in a long relationship where we find that we have held onto grudges. What does it take for us first to forgive ourselves for all of the harmful things we've done or said or held onto, for us to accept and embrace all our feelings of unhappiness and anger as genuinely ours, separating them entirely from our thoughts about our partner. What does it take to feel our feelings as our own—and our own responsibility—and let our partner off the hook? We may still disagree, we may still need to negotiate a new way of doing things, but we are responsible for our feelings, how we hold onto them or act them out.

Can you then, having come to terms with your own feelings, forgive your partner for however they have acted with theirs? Can you reach out with forgiveness and kind feelings – again and again – holding with compassion their treacherous emotions, until they feel safe enough to talk, and then can you talk things through?

Clearly this is not a practice meant for a situation that involves physical abuse. Nor is it appropriate for a situation where it will foster chronic verbal abuse. Better to set appropriate boundaries to prevent the abuse, then do the practice.

One of the benefits of doing the practices of ending suffering using the three intentions, is that we learn at last to live without our endless judgments of ourselves and others. We can't live in the present moment, or access suffering's wisdom without letting go of these judgments. How wonderful!

We change our fate, our future, by simply changing our habits <u>now</u>, just by learning to live in the present moment and practice the three intentions. We don't get away with anything. When we do good deeds, good will follow us. When we do something harmful, we're creating harm inside and out.

1000 Acts of Kindness

I tell myself,

It takes 1000 acts of kindness
to undo one unkind deed.

How difficult it can be to regain someone's trust if we have lied to them, betrayed them, done them harm.

How equally difficult for us if we know we have been a liar or a cheat to feel good about ourselves. It impacts our capacity for intimacy, even if we've never done wrong to our intimate partner. When it's time for us to be most deeply connected to another we will project our own untrustworthiness upon them, and not trust them. We will hide or shut down. Or we will recognize that we are not worthy of the trust and closeness that they bestow upon us and we will become diminished, unable to connect the full force of our being with the full force of theirs. Here we most need forgiveness for ourselves, as we let thoughts go and feelings be. And in the future, how wonderful it is to begin to transform our inclinations to act in harmful ways into acts of wisdom.

Kindness

Reflect for a moment, how much acts of kindness have meant to you. As you live in the present moment, notice these things:

What happens inside you when you go out of your way to do an act of kindness?

What happens when instead you do something thoughtless, unkind? Or you hold yourself back from an intended beneficent action?

What happens when someone does something unkind to you—
inside yourself, moment by moment?

What happens when you experience another's kindness toward you?

> We have misorganized the world. These responses that we have to kindness and unkindness in ourselves and others are more fundamental to life than the laws of physics or mathematics.

What if we paid as much attention in the construction of human society to the subtlest workings of human virtue, kindness and suffering's wisdom as we pay to mathematical laws when we construct our buildings and our bombs? Pay attention. Simply notice what happens inside you and to others as you take up a life of virtue as your primary path. Your understanding of how the universe is constructed and what it is made of will change more profoundly than from studies of the most complex cosmology.

Homework:
Kindness Practice

Take a day—any day—today or tomorrow are as good as any. Don't wait for the right time. Work days are as good as days off. Travel days, visits by your mother-in-law, days of surgery, birthdays, days with the dentist or your accountant, any day will do, but the best day of all is today. Don't wait. Do it now.

So, take today, and whenever an act of kindness arises in your mind, do it! Don't hesitate, don't wait. Go out of your way. All in the context of a normal day, but as you go about your day, when you notice an opportunity to do something kind, do it. And keep your eye out for opportunities.

And at the end of the day, write up what happened.

Changing Habits

It's difficult to change old habits, even to bring kindness into every corner of our lives.

When someone starts to preach about moderation and virtue, it is not unusual for us to want to get up and leave the room. The tension in our body goes up while our thinking mind shuts down. Many of us think that we are quite good enough as we are or that we're as good as we can be, or that significant, lasting improvement is not realistic. Where we have noticed failings in our nature, and we've tried to make a change, after a period of time it seems those failings have come back in spades.

So we don't make serious and sustained efforts in regard to them any more. Our life goes along better if we just don't pay any attention. We think, "That's just the way I am" and we put them out of our mind.

Sometimes when an old uncomfortable habit comes up for us once again, we fill our lives with curses: "I hate myself!" we say intermittently as we move on to other things. We don't look any further at our experience than that.

At other times we beat ourselves up with questions like "Why do I do this?" Or, thinking that we're feeling our feelings, we label

ourselves with messages like this: "I feel like a schmuck" or "I feel
like such a failure." Or we assign ourselves tasks instead of feeling,
with messages like this: "I feel like I should have said something
kind to her."

Of course by now you know that each of these statements embodies
a structure of suffering. Each of them also contains both a judgment
of ourselves and an implicit sense of our responsibility to change,
to act differently in the future, as if we could "fix" everything. So
often when we think we are experiencing a feeling, we are actually
short-circuiting the feeling by expressing a judgment instead which
already contains a message for ourselves of what we must do in
the future to prevent our unfortunate behavior. These are defenses,
structures of resistance as well as structures of suffering. They block
our path. They repress our emotions. What if we let go of the desire
to change the situation or even to change ourselves, and, instead, we
just felt the sadness, the fear or the anger as a meditation, and stayed
more fully inside ourselves, working our way toward suffering's
wisdom? What might happen then?

Or if we are too unsteady and it is too painful to feel and the habit
too alluring, what if we immediately stop playing the images of
temptation out in our minds and give ourselves something else
nourishing and enriching to do right now, and the promise of
something more in the future, some substitute behaviors, gifts to
yourself that you are prepared to give in order to stop your cycle of
destructive behavior. In particular, think of things to give yourself
that nourish your spirit, that make you feel wonderful. Make sure

they are things just as tasty, but in a deeply nourishing sense, as the things you give up. Think of some of the practices you've picked up from Suffering's Wisdom. Give yourself time with your best friend, your children or someone you love. Give yourself a walk on the beach or a stroll through the park. Take a swim or get a massage. Play music. Sing! Drop all of your responsibilities for the time being and do something you really like to do. Promise yourself an evening of meditation or a day of living in the present moment. Give yourself an experience of genuine freedom.

This is how wisdom is gained: consciously transforming our most miserable states into nourishment for the spirit.

How the Husk Falls
from the Seed

Every moment of suffering and every suffering life is a seed of
wisdom. At its end, the husk falls off, all the thoughts and stories we
were attached to, all the judgments and analyses and debates. The
final judgment falls like the husk of a seed, blown away by the wind
or absorbed by the earth, and what is revealed, what is born is life
itself, nothing but spirit and its expression.

I tell myself:

> There is one reason & one reason only why difficult
> things happen to me.
> They happen so I can become a better person. They give
> me the chance to take spiritual action, and to transform
> suffering into suffering's wisdom.

Speech

In our relationships, perhaps nothing requires greater care, and nothing can promote greater good or create greater harm than speech. At the same time speech is riddled with paradox. It is the place where we attempt to speak "the truth" or at least "our truth", but it is seldom a purely conceptual area. After all it is the place where we communicate with each other and has the potential for powerful, if not explosive feelings. As the place where truths may easily collide, it is the place where trust is created and destroyed.

The deeper dilemma here is that speech, by its very nature is always two stages removed from truth, always an abstraction. The truth itself is beyond words. This is why, in inner listening, we practice the observation of feelings and sensations, not thoughts, to come closer to the truth of things. It is not necessarily that feelings and sensations are more true in a moment than a thought might be, but that thought is an abstraction and truth is not. One stage removed from truth is the conceptual realm, the realm of thought. One stage removed from thought is speech. It takes real art to match speech with what is true. It is not always easy to distinguish that art from cunning. Are we speaking the truth, or are we hiding and manipulating language so that the "I" gets what it wants or so that they can't call "me" a liar.

Actually, when we speak, we know in a moment if we have done wrong. We wince, we flinch internally, or we defend our actions with strong statements to ourselves or others.

These are structures of suffering that long for release, but are more likely to be stuffed down inside ourselves, or rehearsed and rationalized in ways that will make them habitual. At this point we know what we must do: let our thoughts go and be fearless and forgiving with our feelings, feeling them as sensations, living in the present moment and pulling the plug on the self.

The path of virtue raises another way of working with suffering, a pro-active way. Instead of waiting for suffering to occur and then responding to it with a practice, take action before suffering ever arises to end it before it's begun.

Try this:

- Speak the truth and only the truth
- Speak kindly or directly, but never harshly
- If you must speak behind someone's back, speak only things they would feel completely comfortable hearing.
- Eliminate vain talk.

Or try this: Whenever you speak, ask yourself:

> Am I truthful?
> Am I thoughtful (of others)?
> Am I mindful (of each moment of my inner experience)?
> Will my speech facilitate the transformation of suffering into wisdom?

Practice these four things and you will know what has integrity and what doesn't, what works and what doesn't work.

The great thing is that we can, by our practice with speech, establish habits and patterns of behavior that bring clarity, peace, kindness and connection into our lives – virtuous cycles, rather than cycles of suffering and ill-ease.

The Fallibility of Speech

One of the wonders of speech is how riddled it is with ethical dilemmas, how the subtlest shifts in tone or phrase can move us from virtuous to unethical behavior. This makes speech into one of our greatest teachers.

For instance:

When someone is struggling in her life and we talk behind her back, is it always merely gossip, or is there a kind of talk that is genuinely and wholeheartedly looking to help? How do we tell the difference?

At work, we may be asked to evaluate a person's performance behind their back. How do we know what is healthy speech then?

If you loved deer and a hunter with a rifle asks you as you walk in the woods, "Did you see the deer? Which way did it go?" Would you tell the truth? What would be the right thing to do?

Many years ago, I was on the verge of being attacked by a pack of wild dogs. Without a second's thought regarding "harsh speech" I stood up and bellowed "Go!" "Get!" "Away!" The dogs stopped in their tracks and then retreated.

How do we know when we've not spoken appropriately? Most of us know without even thinking. It leaves a bad aftertaste. These are feelings we are meant to feel, letting our thoughts go, in order to bring suffering to its end. Once we have brought the feelings to a place of ease, then it's worth looking at our behavior to determine whether we need to make amends for something we've said, or merely understand clearly enough what we've done to make a commitment to ourselves never to do it again.

> To me, the fallibility of speech is not so much a problem, as it is what makes speech endlessly interesting and deeply human—something we can always work with and learn from to eliminate suffering inside ourselves and to bring peace to the world.

Actions

It is said that actions speak louder than words. Just as in speech, in all of our actions it is worthwhile to look and ask ourselves, "Am I harming others?" And stop yourself if the answer is yes. Notice if you rationalize questionable behavior to yourself by saying "They won't notice," "Everyone does it," "It won't matter," "I was in the right." And consider stopping the behavior instead.

Take an inventory of your life. You've noticed how it feels to do harmful actions, notice how it feels instead to hold back from doing them. You may find (beneath a flutter of anxiety), a feeling of transformation, of spaciousness and peace. You might feel as clear as if you'd been meditating all week. In realms of virtue, external actions can be as powerful engines of transformation as years of meditative practice.

Notice how it feels to reach out to your family, friends and neighbors with acts of kindness, with actions that bring blessings into their lives. Living in the present moment, notice clearly the difference inside yourself between these two kinds of actions and their consequences.

Sexual Misconduct

One of the greatest harms done in the world today involves sexual misconduct. Breaking the bond of faith and trust in each other causes our community, our families and our relationships to flounder. Our sexual lives are meant to be a great flourishing of love for our intimate partner. It is indeed the place where two beings become one.

If your sexual life is not flourishing, look to see if you are stuck in inappropriate actions or inactions.

If you are, best to stop and do the three practices instead, finding your way to acts of kindness and light. The harm you are doing to others as well as to yourself is immeasurable. Best to stop right away, get help and move forward with a healthy life.

It is easy to blame our partners when our intimacy begins to fade, but blame is usually a sign of a lack of personal vigor. There's not much you can do about your partner, and a huge amount you can do about yourself. Figure out what a flourishing relationship might look like. If inaction is your problem, start taking actions that will improve your connection with each other. You might start with acts of kindness.

Look particularly at structures of suffering that might be blocking you. As you open to the difficult feelings underneath, find a way to begin conversations with your partner that will restore intimacy to your lives.

> It is a rare relationship that cannot be restored by simple and sustained acts of kindness and a genuine, consistent sharing of deep feelings.

Not that the road won't be tentative, or even rocky, but if you persist with deep feeling and acts of kindness, your chance for success is high, and if you don't succeed, you will nonetheless have profoundly enriched your own life. You will have acted with integrity in the relationship and developed good practices for your future.

Work

The big question about our work is:

Are we doing work that brings us passionately alive, that calls forth from us not merely our vitality, but our good hearts, our creativity and integrity as well?

If our work does not call forth the best in us, why are we doing it? And if we are sacrificing ourselves once again for someone else, or for some far-flung future dream, how long are we willing to sell our souls (and the millions of moments that will never return) for a dollar?

When we create the work we love to do, we live our passion, it becomes second nature to us, we no longer yearn for it, but come alive within it. Our vitality and joy inspires those around us.

If we don't live this completely at work, our selfing and our suffering will follow us wherever we go. If we don't live this completely now, it's still possible to look at how to bring more freedom and more of ourselves into whatever work we do. Consider here, as well, finding a Life Planner in your neighborhood, someone who's been trained to help you discover your most vital life, and to create the financial architecture to make it successful and sustainable.

Work and Practice

It can be hard to practice the ways to end suffering at work. It helps periodically to do an inventory of our experience and choose areas that call out for action or attention.

For instance:

- In what areas do I question my own integrity at work? Where do I hold it without question? Where can I bring more integrity into what I do?
- Where do I feel fresh, vital, and creative at work? Where not?
- When do I have an opportunity to practice kindness at work? What are the repetitive tasks I do? (Even driving or walking halls.) Can I do them as a meditation, pulling the plug on the self, employing the four qualities of *dedication, balance, agility* and *focus*?
- Where do I have the opportunity to be fearless and forgiving in the midst of suffering, whether toward myself or towards others?
- In what encounters or meetings can I make myself into a barometer of feelings, so I know more about what is going on emotionally in the situation and can help facilitate a smoother process?

Make a chart with the three intentions as columns, and your daily activities as rows. Investigate where you already practice them, and where you might improve. You won't be able to do it all at once, so choose an area where it might be easiest to make the change or where the impact would be greatest.

The Three Intentions

Daily Activities	Live in the Present Moment	Pull the Plug on the Self	Be Fearless & Forgiving in the Midst of Suffering
Dressing			
Eating			
Working			
Meetings			
Emails			
Negotiations			
Driving			
Cooking			
Family Time			
Exercising			
Relaxing			

Download a free copy of this worksheet at www.sufferingswisdom.com

We are always serving others in our work. What is the quality
of your service? Map out your day. Where do you take pride in
your work or your relationships with others and where do you
not? Explore how to make your day into a work of art, where equal
attention is placed to the minute articulation of each task and to the
grace and kindness with which it is delivered.

See if you can reframe your work so that you understand that its
primary function is the alleviation of suffering.

Explore your attitudes toward work. Notice where resentment,
blame or complaint diminishes your vitality and do the work
of unlocking these structures of suffering with fearlessness and
forgiveness. You will discover either a new vitality in your job, or an
ability to better decide how to change your circumstances.

Where we seem to suffer most at work is where our egos feel
bruised, where we feel judged by others, or where we've been false
to ourselves in some way. Using the three intentions, see if you can
bring an end to your suffering in those areas, so that you can address
with greater clarity your relationship or integrity issues at work.

If you do enough of this practice, you will find that it can transform
the workplace into a visionary or spiritual landscape, where the
primary work you do is the ending of suffering.

When you find yourself rushing to do something at work, or to get somewhere, remind yourself "I'm already there, I'm already where I want to be, right here in this moment. Life is already complete."

War and Children

There are many excuses for war, but the fundamental cause of
war lies inside ourselves. While our daily focus is preponderantly
on the world outside, we live in inner conflict with no skillful
understanding of the inner world, its emotions or its urges and
desires. As a consequence, when we are angry, rather than
recognizing our anger as a path to suffering's wisdom, we seek
to get rid of it at all costs. We put it outside ourselves, attach it to
something out there. And then, we figure, only by resolving the
conflict externally will the inner conflict go away. As ridiculous as it
sounds, wars thus become the ultimate means of resolving
inner conflict.

If we were sincere about ending war, we would seek to live as deep
inner lives of ending suffering within, as we live engaged lives in the
world. We would seek this for ourselves as well as for
our communities.

We would start by teaching our children the three intentions and the
pathways to end suffering. For it is only when as communities of
beings we have internalized the process of transforming suffering
into wisdom, so that it has become second nature to us, that we will
bring an end to war.

This is not a far-flung dream. Suffering's wisdom can easily be taught
to children as their emotional life begins to deepen and they learn the
difference between a thought and a feeling. Then and only then will wars
end and will our habitual response to suffering be to transform it
into wisdom.

Epilogue

The practices of "Suffering's Wisdom" can be used in the midst of the most excruciating suffering, our own and others, suffering that is unjust, suffering that is unfair, suffering that seems to arise even from evil, to transform that suffering into wisdom. The practices are not meant, however, as an apology for suffering, an excuse for it, nor are they meant as a substitute for the social action we might take to eliminate the external causes of suffering. I speak of them here because, whatever we do in life, however we conduct ourselves, however we protect our children, or our elderly, or our civilization, suffering comes. Suffering happens, and if all our view is outside on its external causes, we will never become wise, and the world itself will not change. If it is to become a world of wisdom, it must change utterly.

There has been such an experience growing inside me throughout this year. From the first idea of "Suffering's Wisdom", something mysterious has been close by. Something wild and unflappable, something with unaccustomed clarity and ease has accompanied me throughout. A sense that somehow comprehends that all of this that surrounds us, as wondrous as it may be, is nothing but false front, a Hollywood set—that all of our senses pick up only the dust and dimes of something not substantial, of cardboard, a show of light and dazzle that, ever changing, sparkles with false wonder, wrapped

around and within by thought until it becomes a world we think is ours or is real. We live in this way deluded, not really knowing where we are, or what we are.

Whereas, in fact, from close observation, from doing the three wise practices, from living in the present moment, from pulling the plug on the self, from being fearless and forgiving in the midst of suffering, we arrive at quite a different experience, one nearly impossible to describe, it is so immense. We find ourselves in a world, not multi-dimensional, but all-dimensional, where nothing is left out, and there is nothing to be added, where everything is complete. A world of clarity and ease, where each sense arises from inside us as if it were the external covering, the detailed painting on the outside of an immense cathedral, as a momentary expression of the depth and immensity within. But the place within is a place we discover we can live. And every action that is taken from this inner place is filled with such grace and power, it is unbreakable. No split between our outward actions and our inner being. No longer inside or outside, just a knowing that this becomes a broken-down, incomplete world when experienced from anywhere else.

The three wise actions end suffering, that is clear. But what occurs when suffering is done? Isn't that the place where the fragrance and the blossom of life itself is begun?

<u>George's Teaching</u>

George has primarily taught two audiences.

For the first, the general public, he's been teaching the practices of transforming suffering into wisdom in small classes and retreats across the US for half his adult life.

The second audience, financial advisors, he's been training professionally in a set of skills that is called Life Planning. This training and related trainings by others have become a movement happening all over the world in financial services. He has been called the father of that movement. The purpose of the movement is to inspire all people, everywhere, advisors and everyone else to live their lives of greatest authenticity and freedom. Part of each training he gives guides his students through the practices of the Structure of Suffering that lead to wisdom. The rest of the training involves helping people discover the way of living that will make their hearts' sing and bring a genuine freedom into their lives, and then inspiring them to live that way and providing a sustainable financial architecture to make it happen.

"That's why my work is with financial advisors." says George. "It is the fastest way I know to solve the age-old conflict between spirit and world."

"From each of these audiences I have received repeated requests to put my teachings down in writing. It is my hope that these pages will help many of you to achieve much greater happiness and wisdom in your lives, just as the practices have helped me and my students."

The world is a large place to bring this work, but when we suffer, the world can seem no larger than our own sorrow.

To learn more about George's teachings on money, please visit the Kinder Institute of life Planning's website at www.kinderinstitute.com.

Other websites

  www.sufferingswisdom.com
  www.georgekinder.com
  www.georgekinderphotography.com

Books by George Kinder

  A Song for Hana, 2007
  Lighting the Torch, 2006
  Seven Stages of Money Maturity, 1999

Made in the USA
Charleston, SC
04 June 2013